"Among many antifaith books you may find Bart Ehrman's *Misquoting Jesus: The Story Behind Who Changed the Bible and Why.* This is a broadside attack upon the Scriptures, and Christians need to be able to rebut it. Thankfully, Dr. Timothy Paul Jones has written *Misquoting Truth,* a scholarly and gracious (but firm) rebuttal to Dr. Ehrman."

D. JAMES KENNEDY, PH.D., SENIOR MINISTER, CORAL RIDGE PRESBYTERIAN CHURCH

"In *Misquoting Truth,* Timothy Paul Jones gives Bart Ehrman's *Misquoting Jesus* and *Lost Christianities* the debunking they deserve. Jones exposes the bias and faulty logic that surface time and again in these highly publicized books. *Misquoting Truth* provides a much needed antidote and will serve students and Christian leaders very well. I recommend this book enthusiastically."

CRAIG A. EVANS, PAYZANT DISTINGUISHED PROFESSOR OF NEW TESTAMENT, ACADIA DIVINITY COLLEGE, AND AUTHOR OF *FABRICATING JESUS: HOW MODERN SCHOLARS DISTORT THE GOSPELS*

"Timothy Paul Jones's writings are always engaging, compelling and often humorous. He captivates me with everything he writes. When I read his writing, I have many 'Aha!' or 'I wish I'd thought of that' moments. This isn't the first great book that Timothy's written, and it won't be the last. Make certain you don't miss it!"

JAMES L. GARLOW, PH.D., COAUTHOR OF THE BESTSELLING *THE DA VINCI CODEBREAKER* AND *CRACKING DA VINCI'S CODE*

"Dr. Jones reminds us that Christians should never be afraid of open debate. With tradition, experience, reason and Scripture as our final measure we can put all ideas on the table with confidence that in the end we will embrace what is true and discard what is false."

EVERETT PIPER, PH.D., PRESIDENT, OKLAHOMA WESLEYAN UNIVERSITY

"Jones clearly refutes in a Christlike manner the claims of *Misquoting Jesus.* A must-read for those who love to give an answer for the faith!"

LIEF MOI, MARS HILL CHURCH CAMPUS PASTOR, SEATTLE, WASHINGTON

"The most radical wing of New Testament scholarship has gotten a disproportionate amount of press in recent years. As representative as any of this trend today is Bart Ehrman, whose books on textual criticism and noncanonical Gospels make it sound as if we have little idea what the New Testament authors originally wrote or little reason to believe that theirs was an accurate, and certainly the oldest, rendition of the life of Jesus and the gospel message. Timothy Jones sets the record straight in this courteous but direct critique of charges about misquoting Jesus and alternate or lost Christianities. Abreast of all the latest and best scholarship, he nevertheless writes in a straightforward, easy-to-read style that any thoughtful layperson can handle. An absolute must-read for anyone confused or taken in by the revisionist biblical historians of our day."

CRAIG L. BLOMBERG, DISTINGUISHED PROFESSOR OF NEW TESTAMENT,
DENVER SEMINARY

"Dr. Jones has written a first-rate book on an essential and timely subject. Both specialists and nonspecialists will benefit from his honest, polite and clearly explained treatment of issues concerning the reliability of the New Testament text and its authorship. In a day of confusion among non-Christians and Christians alike, this is a must-read."

PETER JONES, SCHOLAR-IN-RESIDENCE, WESTMINSTER SEMINARY CALIFORNIA, AND
AUTHOR OF *STOLEN IDENTITY: THE CONSPIRACY TO REINVENT JESUS*

"In *Misquoting Truth,* Timothy Paul Jones has written an informative, creative book that needs to be read by all serious, thinking Christians. It is as informative as it is entertaining, and it will provide a secure foundation for continuing to trust in the accuracy of God's Word. It answers the basic criticisms leveled at the New Testament by Dr. Bart Ehrman, while at the same time providing a proper understanding of the basics of textual criticism. Jones does not skirt the difficult issues, but deals with them head-on, providing careful and balanced answers. I highly recommend this book to those seeking to find answers to the question, 'Can the Word of God be trusted?'"

PAUL D. WEGNER, PROFESSOR OF OLD TESTAMENT, PHOENIX SEMINARY

"Timothy Paul Jones turns the tables on Bart Ehrman's overstated *Misquoting Jesus*. He applies to Ehrman the same probing logic that Ehrman claims to apply to the New Testament evidence. The evidence turns out to be more believable than Ehrman's strained interpretations of it. It is not the New Testament writers or copyists who depart from history, Jones shows, but a few scholars who invest too much faith in their skepticism. Jones not only checks that skepticism: along the way he equips readers to make their own informed choices about authorship, scribal transmission, and church selection (or rejection) of key New Testament passages and documents—and many writings from outside the New Testament as well. This is a valuable primer for orientation in a discussion that cannot be ignored."

ROBERT YARBROUGH, ASSOCIATE PROFESSOR OF NEW TESTAMENT AND NEW TESTAMENT DEPARTMENT CHAIR, TRINITY EVANGELICAL DIVINITY SCHOOL

"It is an unfortunate thing when a scholar uses a technical discipline such as textual criticism to browbeat an unsuspecting public. Timothy Jones's evenhanded approach challenges the overblown claims of Ehrman's sensationalized account of the textual history of the New Testament. Jones agrees with Ehrman at many basic points, but repeatedly challenges his conclusion that the New Testament is untrustworthy, effectively countering each of Ehrman's revisionist claims. In a most readable treatment Jones presents anew the case for the trustworthiness of the New Testament.

"There was a time when F. F. Bruce's little book on the reliability of the New Testament documents was enough. Now new challenges to the integrity of the New Testament have arisen. Timothy Jones rises to meet these new challenges by combining this refutation of Bart Ehrman's book *Misquoting Jesus* with a thorough primer on New Testament textual criticism. Both authors work with the same evidence and share a good deal of common ground, but they arrive at surprisingly different conclusions. In the process of challenging the conclusions of Bart Ehrman's popular book, Jones investigates several alleged 'significant changes' in the text and finds that none of them requires readers to rethink an essential belief about Jesus or to doubt the historical integrity of the New Testament.

"This book is classic apologetics yet without any hint of rancor. Jones writes in a readable conversational style, combining pastoral concern with excellent activities for beginning students as well as entertaining anecdotes and illustrations. The book is autobiographical to a high degree, which increases its personal appeal.

"Written with troubled believers in mind, Jones begins by borrowing a generous definition of inerrancy—*inerrancy* means simply that the Bible tells the truth—a definition which, he says, gives plenty of room for the many extant textual variants. In the end, Timothy Jones suggests that Ehrman lost his faith not because he 'peered so deeply into the origins of Christian faith,' but because he gained his understanding of Christian faith in a fundamentalist evangelical context that allowed little (if any) space for questions, variations or rough edges. Jones does not shy away from these 'rough edges,' but he presents a compelling case that the New Testament text as we have it is a reliable witness to the teachings of Jesus and of the first Christians."

T. SCOTT CAULLEY, D.THEOL., DIRECTOR OF THE INSTITUTE FOR THE STUDY OF CHRISTIAN ORIGINS, UNIVERSITY OF TÜBINGEN, TÜBINGEN, GERMANY

"In recent years, Christians have been assailed by a book genre that is increasingly critical of Christian beliefs. *Misquoting Truth* reminds us that this critical alarm is often sounded in bombastic ways that seldom present the whole picture. Timothy Jones explains why there is no new information in Bart Ehrman's *Misquoting Jesus* that threatens what Christians believe about the New Testament text. Further, he moves the discussion to a shelf where it is accessible to everyone. Numerous practical teaching pointers help the reader to digest the material. The result is a well-integrated volume that accomplishes what few books do: disarming the critics while at the same time connecting with a large range of readers. Bravo, InterVarsity, for publishing yet another excellent volume that communicates crucial truth to this generation!"

GARY R. HABERMAS, DISTINGUISHED RESEARCH PROFESSOR AND CHAIR, DEPARTMENT OF PHILOSOPHY AND THEOLOGY, LIBERTY UNIVERSITY; AUTHOR OF *THE CASE FOR THE RESURRECTION OF JESUS*

MISQUOTING TRUTH

A Guide to the Fallacies of
Bart Ehrman's *Misquoting Jesus*

TIMOTHY PAUL JONES

An online study guide for this book is available at
www.ivpress.com

IVP Books

An imprint of InterVarsity Press
Downers Grove, Illinois

InterVarsity Press
P.O. Box 1400, Downers Grove, IL 60515-1426
World Wide Web: www.ivpress.com
E-mail: email@ivpress.com

InterVarsity Press® is the book-publishing division of InterVarsity Christian Fellowship/USA®, a student movement active on campus at hundreds of universities, colleges and schools of nursing in the United States of America, and a member movement of the International Fellowship of Evangelical Students. For information about local and regional activities, write Public Relations Dept., InterVarsity Christian Fellowship/USA, 6400 Schroeder Rd., P.O. Box 7895, Madison, WI 53707-7895, or visit the IVCF website at <www.intervarsity.org>.

Unless otherwise indicated, quotations from the Christian Scriptures are translated by the author from Eberhard Nestle et al., Novum Testamentum Graece, 27th ed. (Stuttgart: Deutsche Bibelgesellschaft, 1999).

Unless otherwise indicated, quotations from the Hebrew Scriptures are from the New Revised Standard Version of the Bible, copyright 1989 by the Division of Christian Education of the National Council of the Churches of Christ in the USA. Used by permission. All rights reserved.

Unless otherwise indicated, quotations from Greek and Latin texts are translated by the author from primary source materials.

This book is published in association with the Nappaland Literary Agency, an independent agency dedicated to publishing works that are: Authentic. Relevant. Eternal. Visit us on the web at http://www.Nappaland.com.

The map of Paul's third missionary journey in chapter five is used under license from Rose Publishing <www.rose-publishing.com>. The Schøyen Collection photographs are the property of Martin Schøyen and used by permission of Elizabeth Gano Schøyen, librarian for the Schøyen Collection, Oslo and London <www.nb.no/bser/schoyen>.

CSNTM photographs are used by permission of Daniel Wallace, executive director of CSNTM <www.csntm.org>

Design: Cindy Kiple

Images: Bible page: Mike Bentley/istockphoto
Jesus choosing apostles: North Wind Picture Archives]

ISBN 978-0-8308-3447-1

Printed in the United States of America ∞

Library of Congress Cataloging-in-Publication Data

Jones, Timothy P. (Timothy Paul)
  Misquoting truth: a guide to the fallacies of Bart Ehrman's
  misquoting Jesus/Timothy Paul Jones.
      p. cm.
  Includes bibliographical references.
  ISBN 978-0-8308-3447-1 (pbk.: alk. paper)
  1. Ehrman, Bart D. Misquoting Jesus. 2. Bible. N.T.—Criticism,
  Textual. 3. Bible. N.T.—Criticism, Textual—History. 4. Bible.
  N.T.—Manuscripts. I. Title.
    BS2325.J66 2007
    225.4'86—dc22
                        2007015588

P	19	18	17	16	15	14	13	12	11	10	9	8	7	6	5	4	3	2	1
Y	23	22	21	20	19	18	17	16	15	14	13	12	11	10	09	08	07			

To my teachers . . .

My sister Shyre, my parents and Shirley Brown
told me that reading opens doors
into worlds of wonder.
And so I made my way through those doors.

Nancy Swihart told a frightened college freshman
that he didn't have to settle
for walking through doors fashioned by others.
"You're a writer," she said, and I believed her.

T. Scott Caulley and F. Alan Tomlinson
led me into wild and wonderful lands
of ancient peoples whose voices still echo
in fragments of papyrus and pottery and stone.

Mark E. Simpson, Robert W. Pazmiño and Dennis E. Williams
taught me that this knowledge does not matter
unless I share it in ways that transform
the lives of ordinary people.

So here I am
because of who each of you has been
in my life.

CONTENTS

Introduction: *A New Breed of Biblical Scholar?*. 11

PART ONE: WHY THE TEXTS CAN BE TRUSTED 27

1 Truth About "The Originals That Matter". 29

2 Truth About the Copyists 39

3 Truth About "Significant Changes" in the New Testament . 51

4 Truth About "Misquoting Jesus" 67

PART TWO: WHY THE LOST CHRISTIANITIES WERE LOST . . . 79

5 Truth About Oral History 83

6 Truth About the Authors of the Gospels 95

7 Truth About Eyewitness Testimony 107

8 Truth About How the Books Were Chosen 121

Concluding Reflections: *"It Fits the Lock"*. 138

Appendix: *How Valuable Is the Testimony of Papias?*. 147

Acknowledgments 149

About the Author 151

Notes. 153

Subject Index. 170

Name Index 174

Scripture Index. 176

INTRODUCTION
A New Breed of Biblical Scholar?

What good does it do to say that the words are inspired by God if most people have absolutely no access to these words, but only to more or less clumsy renderings of these words into a language? . . . How does it help us to say that the Bible is the inerrant word of God if in fact we don't have the words that God inerrantly inspired? . . . We have only error-ridden copies, and the vast majority of these are centuries removed from the originals.

DR. BART EHRMAN

A new breed of biblical scholar"[1]—that's how *The Dallas Morning News* described Bart D. Ehrman, chair of the Department of Religious Studies at University of North Carolina at Chapel Hill and author of *Misquoting Jesus: The Story Behind Who Changed the Bible and Why.* In part, the newspaper got it right. Ehrman is a respected biblical scholar and a sharp-witted communicator. He excels at making complicated concepts understandable to ordinary people. His books and lectures have moved fields of study such as New Testament textual criticism out of a few obscure seminars for graduate students and onto the shelves of mainstream booksellers.

Ehrman's most popular books have been featured on programs ranging from the *Diane Rehm Show* on National Public Radio to Jon Stewart's *The Daily Show* on Comedy Central. After Jon Stewart described *Misquoting Jesus* as "a helluva book," this treatise on textual criticism shot to the number-one slot on Amazon.com. A *Washington Post* correspondent dubbed *Misquoting Jesus* "one of the unlikeliest bestsellers" of 2006.[2] And indeed it was.

So what's the problem?

Despite the description of Bart Ehrman as "a new breed of biblical scholar," most of what Ehrman has to say isn't new at all. The concepts in his books have been current among scholars for decades. What Ehrman and his editors have done is rework these scholarly conclusions for mass consumption, simplifying the concepts and sensationalizing the titles.

Even this would be no cause for concern if it weren't for how Ehrman presents these conclusions and, in some cases, what he adds to them. According to Ehrman, the New Testament Gospels were not written by Matthew, Mark, Luke or John. As a result—at least from Ehrman's perspective—it's unlikely that any of these documents represents eyewitness testimony about Jesus. What's more, Ehrman implies, the available copies of the New Testament manuscripts are so riddled with errors that it may be impossible to know precisely what the authors said in the first place.

WHY THIS BOOK?

I first ran across Bart Ehrman's books while writing portions of *Answers to "The Da Vinci Code"* and *The Da Vinci Codebreaker,* two responses to Dan Brown's novel *The Da Vinci Code.* Dan Brown's attacks on the historical accuracy of the New Testament were riddled with obvious—even laughable—historical blunders. Ehrman's arguments fell into a completely different category; each argument from Ehrman was intelligent, well-crafted and thoroughly believable. For each hour I spent reading one of Ehrman's books, I spent two hours finding the specific, subtle points at which his assertions fell short.

A few weeks after I finished my portion of *The Da Vinci Codebreaker,* Ehrman's book *Misquoting Jesus: The Story Behind Who Changed the Bible and Why* soared onto the *New York Times* bestseller list, with sales surpassing 100,000 copies. At this point, it occurred to me that most of these 100,000 readers were probably *not* biblical scholars. If it had required so much effort for me—with a firm grasp of biblical languages and degrees in New Testament, church history and spiritual formation—to glimpse the errors in Ehrman's writings, his books could quite easily convince hundreds of thousands of others that the New Testament's testimony about Jesus Christ is unreliable.

Here's how Bart Ehrman's bestsellers *Misquoting Jesus* and *Lost Christianities* describe the New Testament documents:

> Not only do we not have the originals [of the Greek manuscripts of the New Testament], we don't have the first copies of the originals. . . . What we have are copies made later—much later. . . . These copies differ from one another in so many places that we don't even know how many differences there are. Possibly it is easiest to put it in comparative terms: there are more differences among our manuscripts than there are words in the New Testament. . . . We have only error-ridden copies, and the vast majority of these are centuries removed from the originals and different from them . . . in thousands of ways.[3]

If one wants to insist that God inspired the very words of scripture, what would be the point if we don't *have* the very

words of scripture? In some places, . . . we simply cannot be
sure that we have reconstructed the text accurately. It's a bit
hard to know what the words of the Bible mean if we don't even
know what the words are. . . . It would have been no more difficult for God to preserve the words of scripture than it would
have been for him to inspire them in the first place. . . . The fact
that we don't have the words surely must show, I reasoned, that
he did not preserve them for us. And if he didn't perform that
miracle, there seemed to be no reason to think that he per-
formed the earlier miracle of inspiring those words.[4]

The Gospels that came to be included in the New Testament
were all written anonymously; only at a later time were they
called by the names of their reputed authors, Matthew, Mark,
Luke, and John. . . . None of them contains a first-person narrative ("One day, when Jesus and I went into Capernaum . . ."),
or claims to be written by an eyewitness or companion of an
eyewitness.[5]

If I accept Ehrman's reconstruction of the historical record, (1) the
original manuscripts of the New Testament no longer exist, (2) the
available copies of the Greek manuscripts of the New Testament vary
in so many places that, in some cases, it is impossible to reconstruct
the original wording, and (3) the New Testament Gospels didn't
come from Matthew, Mark, Luke or John—they were written anonymously, without the benefit of eyewitness testimony, and the authors'
names were ascribed later.

At first glance, Ehrman's facts seem accurate. It's true that the original manuscripts of the New Testament most likely disintegrated into
dust long ago and that no two surviving copies are identical. And
there *are* more differences between the manuscripts than there are

words in the Greek New Testament. Less certain is whether the Gospels were originally anonymous documents—and, yet, Ehrman is in-

---

KNOW MORE

The New Testament was originally written in the Greek language; the Old Testament was preserved primarily in Hebrew, with some portions written in a related language known as Aramaic.

---

deed correct when he points out that the earliest fragments of the Gospels never mention Matthew, Mark, Luke or John as the authors.

None of this presents a problem for persons who view the Bible, in the words of Bart Ehrman, as "a human book from beginning to end."[6] But, if someone happens to embrace the Bible as something *more* than a human book, Ehrman's conclusions create serious difficulties. Simply put, if Ehrman's conclusions about the biblical text are correct, there is little (if any) reason to believe that my copy of the New Testament accurately describes anything that Jesus said or did.

I have nothing against Bart Ehrman. In fact, I appreciate the way he challenges ordinary people to ask difficult questions about their faith. If my path intersects with Ehrman's path at some point, one of the first sentences to pass through my lips will probably be, *Thank you, Bart Ehrman—thank you for showing people that these issues really do matter.*

At the same time, I disagree strongly with many of Ehrman's conclusions. I believe that the content of Scripture is fully human *and* fully divine. I'm convinced that my copy of the New Testament *does* accurately describe what Jesus said and did. And I believe that such convictions can be rooted not only in my personal faith but also in the testimony of history.

Why do I possess such a passion for helping people to understand why the New Testament writings are reliable? Truth be told, this passion began long before Ehrman wrote his first bestseller. It arose even before my status as an evangelical pastor and author created a vested interest in the accuracy of the New Testament documents. This passion was born on a castoff couch in the library of a small Kansas college where a seventeen-year-old student sat staring out a darkened window, searching for some semblance of truth.

FACT SHEET

Bart D. Ehrman

- Chair of the Department of Religious Studies and James A. Grey Distinguished Professor at University of North Carolina at Chapel Hill

- Ph.D., *magna cum laude,* Princeton Theological Seminary (1985)

- M.Div., Princeton Theological Seminary (1981)

- B.A., *magna cum laude,* Wheaton College (1978)

- Diploma, Moody Bible Institute (1976)

- Author of
   The Orthodox Corruption of Scripture
   Lost Scriptures
   Lost Christianities
   Truth and Fiction in "The Da Vinci Code"
   Misquoting Jesus
   Peter, Paul, and Mary Magdalene

HOW TRUTH FOUND ME

A few fluorescent lights still flickered in the corners of the library, nearly hidden behind towering bookshelves. Other than those four glowing fixtures, the main room of the library was utterly dark. The head librarian had told workers to leave these bulbs illuminated, vainly anticipating that some hapless college student might creep

---

LOOK IT UP

autograph In the academic field of textual criticism, the first or original manuscript of a document.

---

into the stacks after hours to steal a book. From my perspective, this scenario didn't seem particularly likely. Until examination week, most of my fellow students would remain blissfully ignorant of the library's existence. Besides, the library's list of missing items confirmed that most students saw no need to wait until the lights were turned off to filch their favorite books.

After locking the lobby doors, I sank into a well-worn couch, a castoff from some inexplicable moment in the 1970s when the words *stylish* and *avocado green* could appear together without triggering peals of laughter. An uneven stack of books on the table in front of me tossed oblong shadows across a tiled floor. The pile included tomes about the myths of dying deities, textual criticism and the canon of Scripture, rabbinic Judaism, and the history of atheism. During the preceding month, while working the lonely five-hour shift before the library closed each evening, I had struggled through nearly all of these books. With each page, I seemed to choke on ever-deepening doubts about my faith.

Seven weeks into my first semester of Bible college, I whispered as I stared at the haphazard stack of books, *and I don't know if I even believe the Bible anymore.* Unable to bear the frustration any longer, I pressed my face against my fists and wept.

It wasn't as if my professors were attacking the Bible; they weren't. But, with each lecture and reading, my assumptions about the Scriptures—assumptions that I had held since childhood—had crumbled into hopeless fragments.

When I took my seat on the first day of New Testament Survey, I had thought that the Greek and Hebrew texts employed by the translators of the King James Version had been preserved perfectly from the time of the apostles until today. As far as I knew, all the most fa-

---

LOOK IT UP

textual criticism The study of various copies of a manuscript with the goal of determining the wording of the autograph.

---

miliar elements of Christian faith—a dying deity, the resurrection, baptism, the Lord's Supper—were unique to Christianity. Until that moment, I may not always have *lived* my beliefs, but I had never doubted them.

Now, I knew that the ancient world was filled with stories of sacramental meals and ceremonial washings, dying deities and resurrected redeemers. Long before Jesus tumbled into a feed trough in some obscure corner of the Roman Empire, the Persians seemed to have venerated Mithras, a virgin-born deity whose birth was celebrated by shepherds and wise men. And there were Egyptian divinities, worshiped thousands of years before Jesus, who were believed to have died and risen from the dead—Osiris and Adonis, Attis and Horus.

Then, I learned in another class that the original manuscripts of the New Testament had disintegrated into dust more than a thousand years ago and that no two remaining copies of these documents were identical. What's more, the translators commissioned by King James had relied on a Greek New Testament that most scholars now recognized as inadequate—a Greek New Testament that included at least one passage that a Franciscan friar may have forged for political reasons.

Nothing had prepared me for these revelations—and I knew that no one in my church or at home was prepared to deal with such doubts either. If I dared to voice these questions, my words would merely confirm their suspicion that academic study leads inevitably to disbelief.

Now, in my first semester of college, I could no longer blindly embrace the Bible as divine truth. I needed to know *why* and *how*. Why did so many elements of Christian faith seem to be borrowed from other religions? Why were there so many differences between manuscripts of the New Testament? How did scholars know that some Greek manuscripts were more reliable than others? And, if no one had possessed a perfect copy of the Greek New Testament for nearly two millennia, how could my New Testament possibly tell me the truth about God?

My professors would probably have been glad to help me, but I was too timid to admit my doubts to them. And, so, I began to read— not casually flipping through an occasional interesting text, but obsessively consuming book after book during my late-night shifts as student assistant in the library. By the time I found myself sinking into the couch and crying out in the shadows of so many conflicting opinions, I had devoured dozens of volumes from every conceivable perspective—and, still, I didn't know what to believe.

So I did the only thing I knew to do.

I kept at it.

I kept reading everything I could find, searching for some distant glistening of truth. And finally, near the end of my second semester of college, the clouds of doubt began to clear—not all of them and not all at once. But, bit by bit, faith reemerged.

It wasn't the same sort of faith that I had possessed when the semester began. In truth, my faith had grown in the darkness. Now, it

---

THINK IT OUT

"In the New Testament, the *thing* really *happens*. The Dying God really appears—as a historical Person, living in a definite place and time. . . . The old myth of the Dying God . . . comes down from the heaven of legend and imagination to the earth of history. It *happens*—at a particular date, in a particular place, followed by definable historical consequences. We must not be nervous about 'parallels' [in other religions] . . . : they *ought* to be there—it would be a stumbling block if they weren't."[7]

C. S. Lewis

---

was far deeper, far richer and far better equipped to understand what it means to embrace the Bible as God's Word. After seven months of seeking truth, truth finally found me.

Through the writings of C. S. Lewis, I saw that the presence of some elements of Christian faith in other religions doesn't mean that Christianity is false. To the contrary, it means that there is, in every system of faith and every human heart, a yearning—however vague—for one true God who enters into death and triumphs over

---

KNOW MORE

The King James Version of the Bible was translated from a sixteenth-century version of the Greek New Testament known as *Textus Receptus*. The editor of *Textus Receptus,* Erasmus of Rotterdam, used the best Greek texts available to him. Older manuscripts of the New Testament have been discovered since that time.

---

it. What's more, this God may sometimes use fragments of truth in other relitions to reveal his glory to the fullest breadth of humanity.

F. F. Bruce's *The Canon of Scripture* and *The New Testament Documents: Are They Reliable?* convinced me that the authors of the Gospels weren't recording mere myths or legends. They were intentionally writing historical documents. The authors' purposes, to be sure, were theological, but their theology was rooted in real events that had happened in the context of human history.

From the works of Bruce Metzger, especially *The Canon of the New Testament* and *The Text of the New Testament,* I learned how—despite the hundreds of thousands of variants in the Greek New Testament—it's almost always possible to determine the original reading of the text. What's more, I learned that none of these points of textual uncertainty undermines any crucial element of Christian faith.

And, still, I clearly recall the aching emptiness that knotted my stomach during those months of doubt. I remember the frustration I felt when I realized that the answers I heard in church simply weren't enough. Most of all, I will never forget the joy that surged in my soul

In 1515 the Renaissance scholar Erasmus pulled together the best New Testament manuscripts that were available to him. The next year the first published Greek New Testament became available. The original title was *Novum instrumentum Omne,* but the text became known as the *Textus Receptus* ("the Received Text") when an editor declared in 1633, "*Textum ergo habes, nunc ab omnibus receptum*" ("The text, therefore, [this reader] possesses which all now receive").

as a pattern of thoughtful trust replaced the blind faith that I had embraced for far too long.

That's why I'm passionate about what I've written in this book—because I know that blind faith isn't enough. I remember the joy of moving from blind faith to thoughtful trust, and I want you to experience that joy too.

A DEAD END?

As I studied Ehrman's writings, what I found most intriguing was that he once faced a crisis of faith similar to my own—but the results of Ehrman's crisis were radically different. During his sophomore year of high school in Lawrence, Kansas, Ehrman had, in his words, "a bona fide born-again experience."[8] Fascinated with Scripture, the burgeoning scholar earned a diploma in biblical studies at Moody Bible Institute in Chicago before beginning his undergraduate degree at Wheaton College.

At first, Ehrman accepted the view of Scripture that he learned at Moody Bible Institute: the Bible was "inspired completely and in its very words—verbal, plenary inspiration."[9] By the time he entered the master of divinity program at Princeton Theological Seminary, Ehrman was struggling with this understanding of the Bible. He had run across many of the same facts that had triggered such deep doubts in my own soul—the nonexistence of the original manuscripts, differences between early copies of the New Testament and the troublesome difficulty of reconciling certain passages of Scripture.

During his second semester at Princeton, Ehrman wrote a paper in which he attempted to reconcile an apparent historical blunder in Mark 2:26. In this passage, Jesus refers to an event that occurred in the time of "the high priest Abiathar," when in fact the event happened—at least according to 1 Samuel 21:1-6—during the high priesthood of Abiathar's father, Ahimelech. Still holding to his belief in the historical truth of Scripture, Ehrman intended to show that this was *not* a historical error after all. A professor's comment, scrawled on the final page of his research paper, transformed the direction of Ehrman's life.

> At the end of my paper, [the professor] wrote a simple one-line comment that for some reason went straight through me. He wrote: "Maybe Mark just made a mistake." I started thinking about it, considering all the work I had put into the paper, realizing that I had had to do some pretty fancy exegetical footwork to get around the problem, and that my solution was in fact a bit of a stretch. I finally concluded, "Hmm . . . maybe Mark *did* make a mistake."
>
> Once I made that admission, the floodgates opened. For if there could be one little, picayune mistake in Mark 2, maybe there could be mistakes in other places as well. . . . This kind of realization coincided with the problems I was encountering the

more closely I studied the surviving Greek manuscripts of the New Testament.[10]

A few years later, Ehrman was teaching a class at Rutgers University entitled "The Problem of Suffering in the Biblical Tradition." During this time, the remnants of his faith slipped away. Faith had become, in Ehrman's estimation, "a dead end."[11] Today, the former evangelical describes himself as "a happy agnostic." In a recent inter-

---

THINK IT OUT

So do the words of Jesus in Mark 2:26 contradict 1 Samuel 21:1-6? Here's one possible alternative: Mark's reference to "high priest" indicates the position that Abiathar eventually obtained. Abiathar was present in the tabernacle during the incident described in 1 Samuel 21 (see 1 Samuel 22:20), but he didn't become high priest until later.[12]

---

view, Ehrman commented that, when someone dies, that person simply ceases to exist, "like the mosquito you swatted yesterday."[13]

It's not my place to judge whether Bart Ehrman is actually "happy" in his agnosticism, as he claims. And God alone knows why the same sort of crisis that deepened my faith in the truth of Scripture destroyed Ehrman's belief in the Bible's inerrancy. What his story reveals to me, though, is that tough questions about the biblical text can neither be swept under the church rug nor confined to colleges and seminaries.

Uncertainties about who wrote the Bible and why, questions about differences between texts and manuscripts, doubts about the books

---

LOOK IT UP

agnostic (from Greek, *a* ["not"] + *ginōskō* ["to know"]) An individual who believes that it is not possible to know whether God is real.

---

that made it into the Bible and the ones that didn't—these are not issues for pastors and professors alone. These issues matter for *everyone*. They especially matter if you happen to view the Bible as something more than a fallible record of human myths and religious experiences.

With this in mind, let's take a close look at the tough issues that Ehrman has raised. Let's sift through the historical evidence and do our best to decide if, perhaps, there's more to Christian faith than "a dead end" after all.

P A R T 1

WHY THE TEXTS CAN
BE TRUSTED

The New Testament texts *have* changed over the centuries—that much is certain. If you have a difficult time understanding *how* texts changed, try this: Gather a dozen or so people together, and give each person a piece of paper and a writing utensil. Then, ask the group to copy exactly what you say as you say it.

Slowly read aloud a chapter or so from a Scripture that isn't particularly familiar—and don't stop, no matter what! Afterward, collect the papers; after the group leaves, copy a paper of your own from a totally different biblical text than the one you originally read. Then, crumple all the copies and randomly rip small holes in them, discarding the smallest bits of paper. Mix the wadded pieces of paper in a box with some dry sand. (If you have a housecat and you want the results of this experiment to get *really* interesting, leave the box on the floor of your living room for a few days and see what happens.)

A week or two later, regather the same group of people. Give them the box and ask them—without using their Bibles—to reconstruct the original text. After they've created their reconstruction, read the text from your Bible and see how close the reconstruction runs to the original text.

I've engaged in this experiment many times, and the *most accurate* reconstruction that any class has accomplished—it was a group of middle-schoolers, by the way—has been only *70 percent* correct. Barely a C-minus, if I gave grades for the project! In other words, in a highly literate culture, with easily accessible writing materials, electrical lights and eyeglasses, the results were still *30 percent wrong.*

Now, consider the same experiment in a culture where your writing materials are rough pieces of papyrus, quills and ink that's a mixture of charcoal, water and ground gum. Remove all eyeglasses and contact lenses. Then, replace your lamps with candles.

That's how the New Testament was copied.

Inkwell from first century A.D. in which a copyist would have made ink by crushing bits of charcoal in a mixture of water and ground gum. (Photograph of MS 1655/2 courtesy of The Schøyen Collection, Oslo and London.)

How, then, can the New Testament manuscripts *possibly* be accurate? How can anyone still trust that the words in the New Testament represent what the original authors had to say? Have centuries of copying caused the original texts to be twisted until Jesus and the apostles wouldn't even recognize the words that are attributed to them?

Personally, I think the New Testament texts *can* still be trusted. Whether you think I'm right or wrong, will you walk alongside me through the next four chapters? Look with me at some tough questions about the texts. Let's wrestle with the truths that we encounter, and let's see where these truths take us!

1

TRUTH ABOUT
"THE ORIGINALS THAT MATTER"

We have only error-ridden copies [of the New Testament], and the vast majority of these are centuries removed from the originals and different from them . . . in thousands of ways.

BART D. EHRMAN

I slumped in an unpadded pew, half-listening to the morning Bible study. I wasn't particularly interested in what the Bible teacher in this small Christian high school had to say. But, when the teacher commented that the Gospels always reported word for word what Jesus said, I perked up and lifted my hand. This statement brought up a question that had perplexed me for a while.

"But, sometimes," I mused, "the words of Jesus in one Gospel don't match the words of the same story in the other Gospels—not exactly, anyway. So, how can you say that the Gospel-writers always wrote what Jesus said word for word?"

The teacher stared at me, stone silent.

I thought maybe he hadn't understood my question, so I pointed out an example that I'd noticed—the healing of a "man sick of the palsy" in Simon Peter's house, as I recall (Matthew 9:4-6; Mark 2:8-11; Luke 5:22-24 KJV).

Still silence.

Finally, the flustered teacher reprimanded me for thinking too much about the Bible. (In retrospect, this statement was more than a little ironic: A *Bible* teacher in a *Bible* class at a *Bible* Baptist school accused me of thinking too much about the Bible!) What I was doing,

---

LOOK IT UP

inerrancy (from Latin, *in* ["not"] + *errancy* ["in a state of error"]) "The inerrancy of the Bible means simply that the Bible tells the truth. Truth can and does include approximations, free quotations, language of appearances, and different accounts of the same event as long as those do not contradict."[1]

---

he claimed, was similar to what happened in the Garden of Eden, when the serpent asked Eve if God had actually commanded them not to eat from the Tree of Knowledge.

I didn't quite catch the connection between my question and the Tree of Knowledge—but I never listened to what that teacher said about the Bible again. I *knew* that something was wrong with what he was telling me. Still, it took me several years to figure out the truth about this dilemma—a truth which, just as I suspected, had everything to do with the teacher's faulty assumptions about the Bible and nothing to do with Eve or the serpent.

Here's what my Bible teacher assumed: *If the Bible is divinely inspired, the Bible must always state the truth word for word, with no variations.* To question this understanding of the Bible was, from this teacher's perspective, to doubt the divine inspiration of Scripture.

WE HAVE ONLY ERROR-RIDDEN COPIES

Oddly enough, when it comes to differences between biblical manuscripts, Ehrman seems to follow a similar line of reasoning. The crucial difference, of course, is that he is far too intelligent simply to deny that there are variations between the documents. He is fully aware of differences not only between different accounts of the same events but also between the thousands of New Testament manuscripts. Because these variations between biblical manuscripts *do* undeniably exist, the New Testament *cannot* be—in Ehrman's estimation—the inerrant Word of God.

> How does it help us to say that the Bible is the inerrant word of God if in fact we don't have the words that God inerrantly inspired, but only the words copied by the scribes—sometimes correctly but sometimes (many times!) incorrectly?[2]

Ehrman is correct that the original New Testament writings disintegrated into dust long ago. He's also correct that the copies of the New Testament documents differ from one another in thousands of instances. Where Ehrman errs is in his assumption that these manuscript differences somehow demonstrate that the New Testament does not represent God's inerrant Word. The problem with this line of reasoning is that *the inspired truth of Scripture does not depend on word-for-word agreement among all biblical manuscripts or between parallel accounts of the same event.*

In the first place, the notion of word-for-word agreement is a relatively recent historical development. "In times of antiquity it was not the practice to give a verbatim repetition every time something was written out."[3] To be sure, I don't believe that one passage of Scripture

LOOK IT UP

codex, codices (from Latin word meaning "block") Stacks of vellum or papyrus, folded and bound for the purpose of creating a book.

papyrus, papyri (from Greek *papyros*) Plant from which ancient peoples manufactured paper. Papyrus plants stand around twelve feet tall with a stem as thick as a person's wrist. The stems were cut in one-foot sections, then sliced lengthwise in thin strips. Two layers of these slices were placed on top of each other—with the grain of each piece running perpendicular to the one beneath it—then beaten together and dried to form paper.

vellum (from Latin word meaning "pelt") Skin of an animal—usually a calf, sheep or goat—used as a writing surface after being soaked in water, saturated with lime, scraped and dried under tension. Also known as parchment, though vellum is technically a piece of parchment of superior quality.

ever directly contradicts other passages. Yet, when someone asks, Does everything in Scripture and in the biblical manuscripts agree word-for-word? that person is asking the wrong question. The answer to that question will always be a resounding no.

Instead, the question should be, Though they may have been imperfectly copied at times and though different writers may have described the same events in different ways, do the biblical texts that are available to us provide a sufficient testimony for us to understand God's inspired truth?

In other words—supposing that God *did* inspire the original New Testament writings and that he protected those writings from error—

are the available copies of the New Testament manuscripts sufficiently accurate for us to grasp the truth that God intended in the first
century? I believe that the answer to this question is yes.

The ancient manuscripts were not copied perfectly. Yet they *were*
copied with enough accuracy for us to comprehend what the original
authors intended.[4] But, if Ehrman's *Misquoting Jesus* had been the
only book I had read on this subject, I might have reached a radically
different conclusion.

To the casual reader, *Misquoting Jesus* could imply that the early
copyists of the New Testament were careless and lacking in literary
skills. What's more, these scribes were prone to making purposeful
changes in the text for purely theological reasons. After considering
Ehrman's oft-repeated reminder that "there are more differences

---

THINK IT OUT

What do you believe about the New Testament? Is the New Testament inerrant? If so, what does *inerrancy* mean to you? In a journal
record your own beliefs about the New Testament.

---

among our manuscripts than there are words in the New Testament,"[5] I would probably be left with the assumption that the texts
of the New Testament aren't all that reliable after all.

So which is it?

Have centuries of careless copying tainted the texts beyond recovery? Or are the New Testament documents sufficiently reliable for us
to discover the truths that the original authors intended? Before answering these questions, it's necessary for us to gain a foundational
understanding of *how* these texts were preserved in the first place. So,

the focus of this chapter will be to take a look at the ways in which these documents were kept and copied among the earliest Christians.

FOLLOWING JESUS IN THE CHURCH'S FIRST CENTURIES

Suppose that you are a follower of Jesus Christ at some point in the church's first three centuries. (You'll be imagining this possibility several times as you read this book so you might as well really get into it: Find yourself a toga, a quill pen and a piece of papyrus, and learn some impressive-sounding Greek and Latin phrases—like *Sit vis vobiscum*, which means, "May the Force be with you.") You have chosen to entrust your life to this deity who—according to the recollections of some supposed eyewitnesses—died on a cross and rose from the dead. Through baptism, you have publicly committed yourself to imitate Jesus' life. Now, you earnestly desire to be more like Jesus.

But how?

Without easy access to writings about Jesus, how can you learn what it means to follow Jesus?

There are no Christian bookstores in the local marketplace. And, even if you *could* purchase a scroll that contained some of Jesus' teachings, you probably wouldn't be able to read it. Between 85 and 90 percent of people in the Roman Empire seem to have been illiterate.[6]

How, then, can you learn more about Jesus? Besides imitating the lives of other believers, you would have learned about Jesus from written documents. But how, as an illiterate person, would you have learned from these writings?

THE FIRST CHURCH LIBRARIES

It's important to recognize that the writings of the prophets and the apostles were so important to early Christians that, long before they possessed buildings, they maintained a church library of sorts. Dur-

KNOW MORE

By A.D. 180, even the Roman authorities knew how and where Christians preserved their writings. Standing trial in North Africa during a time of persecution, a Christian named Speratus was asked, "What books do you keep in your book-chest?" To this, Speratus replied, "Our books and the letters of Paul, a just man."[7] Moments later, Speratus and eleven fellow believers were beheaded for their faith.

ing the first century A.D.,[8] the Jewish Scriptures as well as the writings of the apostles circulated as scrolls—as strips of parchment or papyrus, rolled around a stick.

Your congregation would have kept these scrolls in an *armarion* or "book-chest."[9] Similar book-chests were already common fixtures in Jewish synagogues, where they were called the *'aron* ("chest" or "shrine"),[10] and perhaps in the homes of wealthy Romans. Your church's chest would probably have remained in the home where your church most often gathered. In this book-chest—equipped with specially niched shelves to hold documents securely[11]—sacred writings were organized and preserved for future generations of believers. It is possible, though not certain, that book titles were written on small scraps of parchment or papyrus and sewn along the edges of these documents.[12]

In the late first century A.D., Christians still preserved their writings in book-chests, but these writings began to take a new form: Stacks of papyri were folded and bound to form a codex, the ancestor of the modern book.[13] Codices—that's the plural form of *codex*—were cheaper and more portable than scrolls. Partly because churches owned no buildings and sometimes needed to move their meeting places, the codex quickly became a popular choice for copying the earliest Christian writings.[14]

By the mid-second century, your church's book-chest could have included a few codices that other congregations didn't possess—perhaps a letter to the Hebrews, two letters from Peter instead of one, or a series of visions known as *The Shepherd of Hermas*. Yet most of the codices in your book-chest would be the same ones that other Christian communities used. There would have been a copy of the Septuagint—the Greek translation of the Jewish Scriptures—as well as

---

LOOK IT UP

Septuagint (from Latin, *septuaginta*, "seventy") Greek translation of the Jewish Scriptures, completed between the third and the first century B.C. The designation Septuagint stems from a spurious legend that seventy—according to some versions of the story, seventy-two— scholars worked separately to translate the Septuagint and that, after seventy-two days, all the scholars emerged with identical translations.

---

twenty or so undisputed writings that could be connected to apostolic eyewitnesses of the resurrected Jesus.

Thirteen letters from Paul would likely have been among the oldest copies in your cabinet, then the Gospels of Matthew, Mark, Luke and John, and then perhaps a letter from the apostle Peter and at least one letter from John.[15] When your congregation gathered each week, one of the literate believers would have read passages from the Jewish Scriptures—primarily from the prophets since Christians believed these writings pointed most clearly to Jesus—and from the writings that were connected to the apostles.[16]

But where would the writings in your church's book-chest have come from? Most likely, none of these codices would have come directly from Paul or Matthew, Peter or John! Your church's codices

---

KNOW MORE

What happened to the autographs of the New Testament texts? Around A.D. 200, Tertullian of Carthage claimed that the churches of Corinth, Philippi, Thessalonica, Ephesus and Rome still possessed Paul's original letters.[17] In time, the autographs became worn, so they were replaced and discarded.[18]

---

would have been *copies,* and these copies would have been passed to your congregation from copyists or scribes.

The first Christian copyists were, it seems, simply Christians who were capable of writing. Some of them may have copied scrolls in the Jewish synagogues before they became believers; others may have reproduced Roman legal documents.[19] At some point—probably in the second century[20]—churches in major cities established official groups of copyists to duplicate the Christian Scriptures. And, so, the accuracy of the New Testament documents depended on hundreds of anonymous copyists—men and women whose names you will probably never know.

This, of course, brings up some difficult questions—questions that deserve to be answered: How scrupulous were these copyists? How seriously did they take the crucial task of copying the words of Scripture? And how skilled were they in the first place? Those are the questions that will form the framework for our study in the next chapter, "Truth About the Copyists."

KNOW MORE

At least two descriptions of early Christian worship have survived—one from a Roman persecutor of Christians named Pliny the Younger and another from a defender of Christianity named Justin.[21]

They meet on a fixed day before dawn and sing responsively a hymn to Christ as to a deity. They bind themselves by oath, . . . not to commit fraud, theft, or adultery, nor to falsify their trust, nor to refuse to return a trust when called upon to do so. When this is finished, it is their custom to dismiss and to assemble again to partake of food—ordinary and innocent food. (Pliny)

On the day called Sunday, all who live in cities or in the country gather together to one place, and The Reminisces of the Apostles or the prophets' writings are read, as long as time permits. When the reader has ceased, the person presiding verbally instructs, and encourages the imitation of these good things. We all rise and pray; when our prayer is ended, bread and wine and water are brought, and the person presiding offers prayers and thanksgivings . . . and the people say, "Amen." There is a distribution to each person, and they participate in the food over which thanks have been given. A portion is sent by the deacons to those that are absent. Those that are well-to-do and willing give . . . [to help] the orphans and widows, the ill and those in need. (Justin)

2

TRUTH ABOUT THE COPYISTS

*Christianity . . . is a textually oriented religion whose
texts have been changed, surviving only in copies that
vary from one another, sometimes in highly significant ways.*

BART D. EHRMAN

In *Misquoting Jesus,* Ehrman makes the point that, in the ancient
world, some *professional* copyists may have been barely literate. In
fact, in a court case in Egypt, one copyist declared that another copyist was literate simply because the other copyist was capable of sign-
ing his own name![1] To complicate matters further, Ehrman brings up
some ancient charges against the Christians from the pagan writer
Celsus. Here's what Celsus had to say about the Christian Gospels:

> Some believers, as though from a drinking bout, go so far as to
> oppose themselves and alter the original text of the Gospel
> three or four or even several times, and they change its charac-
> ter to enable them to deny difficulties in face of criticism.

So how sloppy *were* these early Christian copyists? And did they—
as Celsus seems to suggest—purposely change their sacred texts to
deny difficulties about their faith?

In the first place, Ehrman's rendering of the text from Celsus is a bit confusing. Here's an alternate version of this text that captures Celsus' intent with a bit more accuracy:

Some believers, like persons who lay violent hands on themselves in drunken rage, have corrupted the Gospel from its original wholeness, into threefold, fourfold, and manifold editions, and have reworked it so that they can answer objections.[2]

Ehrman views this quotation as evidence of "poor copying practices among Christians."[3] Viewed in its context, though, the quotation from Celsus has little to do with variations among New Testament texts. Celsus' reference to "three or four" most likely refers to the fact that the Christian Scriptures included not one account of Jesus' life but "three or four"—the writings known today as Matthew, Mark, Luke and John.

If this was the case, Celsus may have wrongly assumed that, at one point, there had been a single account of the ministry of Jesus and that Christians had altered this account until three or four distinct Gospels were in circulation. If so, what Celsus missed in his charge was the fact that the New Testament Gospels are not *competing* descriptions of the life of Jesus. The Gospels are *complementary* accounts, each one conveying the same story but with a slightly different perspective of Jesus.

And yet, Ehrman's primary point still stands: It is clear from many ancient sources that the New Testament writings were *not* copied perfectly. A Christian leader named Origen of Alexandria complained in the third century about how carelessly some copyists had duplicated the Scriptures. While preparing his commentary on the Gospel of Matthew, Origen fumed:

The differences between the manuscripts have become great, either through the negligence of some copyists or through the perverse audacity of others; they either neglect to check over what they have transcribed, or, in the process of checking, they make additions or deletions as they please.[4]

Origen's comment does not represent a scientific analysis of the status of New Testament manuscripts in the early third century; it is an exclamatory side-note, evidently uttered in a moment of frustration.

But variations obviously *did* exist among the manuscripts. From the comments of Origen and others, it's clear that the New Testament texts were not being copied perfectly—and that not all changes were accidental.

Since the copyists were fallible human beings, the presence of these differences shouldn't surprise us. The copyists were just as prone to imperfect attention spans, poor eyesight, fatigue and temptations to make unneeded changes as you or I. Occasionally, copyists did change or add words on purpose, usually to clarify something that seemed vague to them. But these changes resulted in *more* confusion by introducing disagreements between the various texts. This is probably why the closing chapter of the Revelation includes a warning to copyists:

I testify to all the ones hearing the words of the prophecy of this book: If anyone adds upon them, God will add upon that person the plagues written in this book; if anyone takes away from the words of the book of this prophecy, God will take away that person's portion from the tree of life and out of the holy city written in this book. (Revelation 22:18-19)[5]

The author of Revelation—believing that this book was a direct

revelation from God—was cautioning future copyists *not* to introduce changes into this document.

Despite such warnings, copyists *did* introduce changes—sometimes intentionally, most often unintentionally. In fact, as Ehrman
points out, the 5,700 or so New Testament manuscripts that are
available to us may differ from one another in as many as 400,000
places—and there are only 138,000 or so words in the Greek New
Testament in the first place![6]

These copyists were also dealing with *scriptio continua*—texts that
included no punctuation, no spaces and no distinction between up-
percase and lowercase letters. (Which provides the context for my favorite quotation from *Misquoting Jesus:* "This kind of continuous writing . . . could make it difficult at times to read, let alone understand,
a text. . . . What would it mean to say *lastnightisawabundanceon-
thetable?* Was this a normal or supernormal event?" The answer
would depend, I suppose, on whether Ehrman is thinking of "abundance" or "a bun dance"—and what sort of buns he had in mind!)[7]
No chapter or verse designations existed either. In fact, three centuries would pass before anyone added such divisions to the texts; even
then, the chapters and verses would not become standardized for another thousand years.

At this point, it may seem as if centuries of careless copying have
tainted the New Testament texts beyond recovery. After all, if there
are more differences among the manuscripts than there are words in
the New Testament, doesn't that mean that recovering the original
words of Paul and the other apostles is a hopeless fantasy? If that's
how you feel, don't give up yet! There are still some truths that we
haven't explored—three facts that, from my perspective, Ehrman's
writings downplay.[8]

(1) First, the vast majority of the changes in the New Testament

documents are not even noticeable when the text is translated into other languages. (2) What's more, it's almost always possible—through a discipline known as textual criticism—to compare manuscripts and to discover where and when changes were made. (3) Perhaps most important, the copyists were more concerned with preserving the words of Scripture than with promoting their own theological agendas.

ARE THE CHANGES SIGNIFICANT?

In the first place, *Misquoting Jesus* grossly overestimates the significance of the differences between the manuscripts. Ehrman's estimate of 400,000 variants among the New Testament manuscripts may be numerically correct—but what Ehrman doesn't clearly communicate to his readers is *the insignificance of the vast majority of these variants.*

Most of these 400,000 variations stem from differences in spelling, word order, or the relationships between nouns and definite articles—variants that are easily recognizable and, in most cases, virtually unnoticeable in translations! For example, the Greek words for "we" (*hēmeis*) and the plural "you" (*hymeis*) look very similar, and copyists frequently confused them. But does it ultimately matter whether "you . . . are children of promise" or "we . . . are children of promise" (Galatians 4:28)?

In other cases, a text literally translated from Greek might have a definite article before the noun. In some manuscripts of John 3:3, for example, the verse—translated very literally—begins, "Answered, the Jesus and said to him . . ." In other Greek manuscripts of the same verse, the definite article is missing. But, since English never places *the* in front of a proper noun anyway, this difference isn't even observable in any English translation! Regardless of the presence or absence of the article, the clause is translated into English as, "Jesus answered and said to him" or some similar wording. In the end, more than 99 percent of the 400,000 differences fall into this category of virtually unnoticeable variants![9]

Of the remaining 1 percent or so of variants, only a few have any significance for interpreting the biblical text. Most important, *none* of the differences affects any central element of the Christian faith. Yet Ehrman continues to declare in *Misquoting Jesus* and in radio and television interviews, "There are lots of significant changes"[10]—a claim that the manuscript evidence simply does not support.

TEXTUAL CRITICISM 101

The science of textual criticism is not—despite the way the name strikes our ears—concerned with criticizing the biblical text. In this context, *criticism* means "analysis" or "close investigation." The task of the textual critic is to look closely at copies of ancient documents and to determine which copy is closest to the original document.

Here's what textual criticism assumes: *It's impossible for all the copyists to have made the same mistake at the same time.* In other words, since changes creep into the manuscripts one at a time in different times and places, it is possible to compare several manuscripts to discover *when* and *where* the error occurred. The textual critic can then, in most cases, figure out the original wording of the text.

Let's look at a simple example of this process. In most Greek manuscripts John 1:6 reads something like this: "There was a man, having been sent from God, whose name was John." But, in a manuscript known as Codex Bezae or simply as D, the text reads, "There was a man, having been sent from the Lord, whose name was John."

Like most differences between manuscripts, this variant doesn't affect the meaning of the text. Still, it's important for scholars and translators to determine which words appeared in the original text of the Gospel of John. So, how do they know which reading is closest to the original?

Let's look at a few manuscripts and decide for ourselves!

Codex Bezae is a vellum codex that includes not only Greek text but also Latin. Together, the style of writing, the use of vellum instead of papyrus, and the presence of Greek *and* Latin in the text suggest that Codex Bezae—the manuscript that reads "sent from *the Lord*"— was copied around A.D. 500. Codex Bezae also seems to have originated in the region of Europe now known as France.

The two primary manuscripts that agree on the other reading— "sent from God" instead of "sent from the Lord"—are a vellum codex

---

LOOK IT UP

uncial (from Latin term for the width of a printed character that occupies one-twelfth of a line) Style of writing popular from the third until the eighth century A.D. Many important manuscripts of the New Testament—including Codex Sinaiticus and Codex Vaticanus— were written in uncial letters.

---

known as Codex Sinaiticus and a papyrus codex that scholars have dubbed $\mathfrak{P}^{66}$. Codex Sinaiticus was copied around A.D. 330. $\mathfrak{P}^{66}$ probably dates from the late second century A.D., a century or less from the time when most scholars believe the Gospel of John was originally written! Codex Sinaiticus and $\mathfrak{P}^{66}$ also seem to have been copied in two different areas of Egypt.

So—from what you've learned in the previous paragraphs— which words do you think John originally wrote? "Sent from *God*" or "sent from *the Lord*"? Make your choice before proceeding to the next paragraph!

Given the agreement between Codex Sinaiticus and $\mathfrak{P}^{66}$—manuscripts that were copied in two different places, more than a century apart—and the fact that these two codices are centuries older than Codex Bezae, nearly every textual critic has concluded that John 1:6 originally read "sent from God." At some point, probably somewhere in Europe in the fifth century, a tired or careless scribe wrote "Lord" (Greek, *kyriou*) when the word should have been copied was "God" (Greek, *theou*).

Now, I must admit to you that most textual issues are far more complicated than the scenario I've presented here. Still, there are cer-

---

KNOW MORE

Codices of New Testament manuscripts are often named to connect them to their place of discovery (Codex Sinaiticus was discovered near Mount Sinai) or to their source (Codex Bezae was once the property of Theodore Beza). These codices may also be given a letter designation, such as A or B or D.

---

tain principles that, with rare exceptions, allow textual critics to determine the original form of the text. Ehrman is well aware of these principles. (In fact, one of Ehrman's former professors—Bruce M. Metzger—is responsible for refining many of the most important principles of textual criticism.) At one point in *Misquoting Jesus,* Ehrman even acknowledges, "I continue to think that even if we cannot be 100 percent certain about what we can attain to . . . , that it is at least possible to get back to the *oldest* and *earliest* stage of the manu-

KNOW MORE

Papyrus codices are usually designated with a $\mathfrak{P}$ followed by a number, such as $\mathfrak{P}^{52}$ or $\mathfrak{P}^{66}$. Sometimes other letters are added to indicate the source of a piece of papyrus. For example, P.Oxy. refers to papyrus fragments discovered near Oxyrhynchus in Egypt.

script tradition for each of the books of the New Testament."[11] In another place, he admits:

> The more manuscripts one discovers, the more the variant readings; but also the more the likelihood that somewhere among those variant readings one will be able to uncover the original text. Therefore, the thirty thousand variants uncovered by [eighteenth-century textual critic John] Mill do not detract from the integrity of the New Testament; they simply provide the data scholars need to work on to establish the text, a text that is more amply documented than any other in the ancient world.[12]

And yet it seems that Ehrman wants—in the words of one reviewer—"to have his text-critical cake and eat it, too."[13] Only a few pages after affirming that it *is* possible to recover the most ancient form of the manuscripts, Ehrman refers to Christianity as "a textually oriented religion whose texts have been changed."[14] Despite admitting that it is possible to recover the "*oldest* and *earliest*" manuscript traditions, Ehrman finds space before the closing paragraphs of *Misquoting Jesus* to repeat his charge that, "given the circumstance that [God] didn't preserve the words, the conclusion seemed inescapable to me that he hadn't gone to the trouble of inspiring them." [15] Yet Ehrman remains well aware that textual critics can, in his words, "reconstruct the oldest form of the words of the New Testament with reasonable (though not 100 percent) accuracy."[16]

Textual criticism isn't a perfect science, but God has worked through more than a few imperfect tools throughout history—Noah and Abraham, Moses and Elijah, Esther and Mary Magdalene, Peter and Paul, the author of the book that you're reading right now. Yet Ehrman seems to expect God to work *around* humanity to preserve his words, so that textual criticism wouldn't even be necessary. The pattern throughout the Hebrew and Christian Scriptures reveals a different pattern—the pattern of a God who works *through* humanity. Given God's penchant for revealing his glory through failure-prone implements of flesh and blood in the first place, who's to say that a process such as textual criticism might not be precisely the pathway that God has chosen to preserve and to restore the words of Scripture?

FOOL AND KNAVE! LEAVE THE OLD READING!

It is important, finally, to remember that the copyists were more concerned with preserving the words of Scripture than with promoting their own theological agendas. Despite his reservations about the earliest Christian scribes, even Ehrman acknowledges this fact in *Misquoting Jesus:*

> It is probably safe to say that the copying of early Christian texts was by and large a "conservative" process. The scribes . . . were intent on "conserving" the textual tradition they were passing on. Their ultimate concern was not to modify the tradition, but to preserve it for themselves and for those who would follow them. Most scribes, no doubt, tried to do a faithful job in making sure that the text they reproduced was the same text they inherited.[17]

In other words, early Christians wanted future generations to find the same truth in the New Testament documents that the first generations of believers had experienced. So, their intent was to hand on to their successors the same text that they received.

This is evident in the complaint from Origen of Alexandria that I quoted earlier. Even though significant differences between manuscripts accounted for no more than 1 percent of the variants, Origen of

This image, discovered in the house of Paquius Proculus in the ruins of Pompeii, depicts two methods of writing in the first century A.D. Some writings were preserved in wooden tablets with wax-coated panels; words were scratched into the wax using styluses like the one in the woman's hand. Other writings were preserved in scrolls, such as the one in the man's hand. In the later first century, codices—ancestors of modern books—began to replace scrolls.

Alexandria considered the differences he saw in his own copies of the Gospels to be "great"! Why? He earnestly desired to see the oldest readings preserved. As a result, even small changes in the text troubled him.

Most copyists seem to have regarded the text with the same reverence that Origen displayed. When one copyist changed the wording of a text in a fourth-century manuscript known as Codex Vaticanus, a later copyist rewrote the original word and added this marginal note: "Fool and knave! Leave the old reading, don't change it!"[18] Certainly, copyists did alter the text from time to time—but the consistency of the available manuscripts of the New Testament demonstrates that these alterations were *exceptions,* not the rule.

So what about the supposed "significant" alterations that Ehrman stresses so heavily in *Misquoting Jesus?* Did copyists actually alter the

---

THINK IT OUT

Sir Frederic Kenyon, former director of the British Museum, once commented concerning the Gospels, "The interval between the dates of the original composition and the earliest extant evidence [is] so small as to be negligible, and the last foundation for any doubt that the Scriptures have come down to us substantially as they were written has now been removed."[19]

---

texts to strengthen scriptural support for their own theological agendas? If so, how does this affect our translations of the Bible today? In chapters three and four, we'll look at most of the supposed "significant" changes that Ehrman lists—as well as a handful that Ehrman doesn't mention at all—and determine what those changes mean for us today.

3

Truth About
"Significant Changes"
in the New Testament

Once a scribe changes a text—whether accidentally or intentionally—then those changes are permanent in his manuscript (unless, of course, another scribe comes along to correct the mistake). The next scribe who copies that manuscript copies those mistakes (thinking they are what the text said), and he adds mistakes of his own. . . . Mistakes multiply and get repeated; sometimes they get corrected and sometimes they get compounded. And so it goes. For centuries.

Bart D. Ehrman

When I need to get information to several hundred people, I type a document on my notebook computer. I then send the document to a printer, walk across the hall from my office and place the original document in the photocopy machine.

After I press the button that's marked "Start Copy," red lights begin to flash and error messages appear, informing me that I've jammed the copier. After opening the machine and contorting my torso into several less-than-dignified positions, the phantom jam remains a menace. At this point, a secretary walks into the room and—somehow being unable to overlook the fact that my head is inside the copy machine while my posterior is protruding from a portion of the photocopier that's been designated for cardstock paper—rolls her eyes and asks, "Did you break the copier again?"

I consider telling her that I was merely checking the ink level in the copier. But I've tried this before, only to be informed that the new copiers don't *have* ink in them. The technician that fixed the copier last time it malfunctioned told me that the new copiers shoot laser beams through a substance that looks suspiciously like gunpowder, which is actually fuel for a thermonuclear warp-drive reactor . . . or something like that.

I climb out of the copier, wipe the warp-drive fuel from my forehead and get out of the way. In a matter of seconds, the secretary has dislodged the jammed scrap of paper, made the photocopies and reminded me to stay out of the copy room. For a church secretary, she sure knows a lot about warp-drive reactors, let me tell you. I know nothing about warp drives except what I've learned from *Star Wars,* which is that warp drives eventually begin to work if you yell at Chewbacca to bring you the hydrospanners. Unfortunately, nobody in my office is named Chewbacca, and everyone seems a little embarrassed whenever I stand in front of the copier and scream, "Chewie, bring me the hydrospanners!" This may be why I've been told to stay out of the copy room.

And so, now, I *do* stay out of the copy room . . . most of the time.

That's how documents are created and copied in the twenty-first century: A computer sends them to a printer; then, after having its buttons punched, its platens unjammed and its warp-drive fuel replenished, a copy machine spits out hundreds or even thousands of

---

KNOW MORE

If possible, refer to a New Testament that includes extensive textual notes as you read chapters three and four. In such a text, you will find notes that say, for example, "some ancient manuscripts omit this verse," or "some ancient manuscripts add this phrase."

---

exact copies of the original document.

This is *not*, however, how documents were created or copied when Jesus and Peter and Paul walked this planet's dusty paths.[1] Documents were, as we have seen, copied by hand. Because documents were hand-copied, there have been thousands of changes in the Greek manuscripts of the New Testament—as Ehrman has rightly pointed out. Most of these alterations were accidental, and they have no bearing on the texts' ultimate significance. Other changes were deliberate, and the theological controversies faced by the copyists motivated at least a few of these intentional alterations.

Up to this point, I find myself vigorously nodding in agreement with Ehrman. From this point onward, though, the common ground begins to fade. According to Ehrman,

> Christianity . . . is a textually oriented religion whose texts have been changed, surviving only in copies that vary from one another, sometimes in highly significant ways. . . . It would be wrong . . . to say—as people sometimes do—that the changes in our text have no real bearing on what the texts mean or on the theological conclusions that one draws from them. . . . In some instances, the very meaning of the text is at stake.[2]

Some of these changes are, Ehrman contends, so significant that they

---

KNOW MORE

So how do New Testament scholars choose the reading of a text that most probably represents the original writing, especially when there are several possibilities? Here are basic principles that most textual critics follow:

1. Look *beyond* the manuscript (a) at which reading is *oldest,* (b) at which reading is supported by texts that were separated by the *farthest distance* and (c) to which *textual family* the manuscript belongs.

2. Look *within* the manuscript for which reading is more probable based on (a) what a copyist would be most likely to change, (b) which possible reading is shortest, (c) which reading might have been an attempt to harmonize one text with another and (d) what difficult words a copyist might have replaced with simpler ones.

3. Look at *other writings* by the same original author to see which reading is most similar to the author's other writings.

"affect the interpretation of an entire book of the New Testament."[3]

From my perspective, a *significant alteration* would be one that requires Christians either to rethink a vital belief about Jesus Christ—a belief that we might find in the Apostles' Creed, for example—or to doubt the historical accuracy of the New Testament documents. Yet, when I look at the changes in the Greek manuscripts of the New Testament, I find *no* "highly significant" alterations.

THE SEARCH FOR SIGNIFICANT CHANGES

In almost every instance, it is possible—as Ehrman himself admits—to "reconstruct the oldest form of the words of the New Testament with reasonable (though not 100 percent) accuracy," recovering "the *oldest* and *earliest* stage of the manuscript tradition for each of the books of the New Testament."[4]

But what about the times when it *isn't* possible to be 100 percent certain about the original form of the text?

It is at this point that Ehrman finds changes that are supposedly so significant that they affect entire books of the Bible. And, it is at this point that I must respectfully disagree with Ehrman. Here's what I find as I look at the textual evidence: *In every case in which two or more options remain possible, every possible option simply reinforces truths that are already clearly present in the writings of that particular author and in the New Testament as a whole; there is no point at which any of the possible options would require readers to rethink an essential belief about Jesus or to doubt the historical integrity of the New Testament.* Simply put, the differences are *not* "highly significant." This is the crucial point where, from my perspective, the evidence does not support Ehrman's conclusions.

With this in mind, let's look at two dozen or so key places where New Testament manuscripts disagree. With a few possible exceptions, these are *not* places where a copyist simply misheard or misread a text. These are texts that, for one reason or another, one or more ancient copyists *changed*. So, grab a translation of the Bible that includes notes about textual differences, and look carefully at the possibilities. Weigh each possibility carefully, and decide for yourself whether the changes are really "highly significant" after all.

THE CASE OF OVER-ZEALOUS COPYISTS

Many noticeable changes in the New Testament documents stem from over-zealous copyists who felt it was necessary to clarify concepts that the texts already taught. For example, in nearly all New

Testament manuscripts, Matthew 1:16 reads something like this: "Jacob was father of Joseph husband of Mary, out of whom Jesus—the one who is called the Messiah—was born." But, at some point, a copyist wanted to make certain readers understood that Jesus was virgin-born, so the scribe changed the verse to read, "Jacob was father of Joseph, to whom was betrothed the virgin Mary from whom Jesus—the one who is called the Messiah—was born."

Though the copyist's actions weren't necessarily commendable, this change doesn't affect anyone's understanding of the text. The remainder of this chapter already affirms that Mary was a virgin when Jesus was conceived (Matthew 1:18-25), so the copyist simply emphasized a truth that was already clear in the text.

Other examples of this sort of change may be found in other texts: In Matthew 17:12-13, a copyist rearranged a couple of words to make certain the reader recognizes that Jesus, not John the Baptist, was "the Son of Man." In Luke 2:33, a scribe seems to have skipped the words "his father" to make certain the readers remember that—though Joseph was Jesus' *legal* father—Joseph was not Jesus' biological father. That assertion is, however, already clear in other passages in this Gospel (Luke 1:26-38; 2:5).

Another example of this sort of alteration can be found in 1 Timothy 3:16. A copyist of this text changed the word "who" to "God"—a change that may have been a copying error, since only a single minute line distinguishes the abbreviation for God (ΘC) from the Greek word that's translated "who" (OC). It's also possible, though, that a well-meaning copyist wanted to emphasize the deity of Jesus Christ. This change was made at a time when the letters attributed to Paul—epistles that described Jesus as being, in some sense, divine (Philippians 2:6; Colossians 1:15)—had already circulated as a complete collection for at least a couple of centuries.

As such, the truth was already present in the copyist's texts. Once again, an over-zealous copyist was merely highlighting a truth that other texts already taught.

You can find two more clauses of this sort in Acts 8:37. Then again, depending on which translation you're using, you may *not* be able to find Acts 8:37, which is precisely the point. If you read the book of Acts as a whole, it's clear that whenever someone was baptized that person also committed his or her life by faith to Jesus Christ (see Acts 2:38-41; 8:12; 9:17-20; 16:14-15, 30-33; 18:8). But, in the most ancient and most reliable versions of Acts 8, the personal faith-commitment of one individual—a eunuch from Ethiopia—isn't particularly clear. Here's how the original version of the encounter between Philip and the eunuch ends:

> The eunuch exclaimed: "Look! Water! What prevents me from being baptized?" He commanded the chariot to stop, and they both went down into the water—Philip and the eunuch—and he baptized him.

At some point, a copyist of this text seems to have been afraid that someone might think the eunuch received baptism without believing in Jesus. So, the scribe added the sentences that became Acts 8:37: "Philip said, 'If you are trusting with your whole heart, you may.' He replied, 'I trust Jesus Christ, God's Son.'" A beautifully rendered text, to be sure—but not one that appeared in the original manuscript of the Acts of the Apostles. Again, the copyist made explicit in a specific text what was already implicit in the book as a whole.

It's possible that the same sort of change occurred in John 1:18. This verse may have originally described Jesus as "the one and only Son." Or the text might have read "the one and only God"—the manuscript witnesses to these two readings are, in my opinion, evenly divided. Here's what is most important, though: *Both wordings affirm truths that are clearly expressed throughout John's Gospel.*

In support of "one and only God," John 20:28 unambiguously identifies Jesus as God, and the opening verses of John's Gospel also imply that Jesus was uniquely divine.[5] In support of "one and only Son," the familiar words of John 3:16 already refer to Jesus as "the only begotten Son" or "the one and only Son." Both readings of John 1:18 fit the larger context of the Gospel According to John. Even though authentic differences *do* exist among the manuscripts, neither possibility contradicts John's Gospel or the remainder of the New Testament, and the differences do not call into question any crucial aspect of Christian faith. If some scribe *did* change "one and only Son" to "one and only God," the scribe simply emphasized a truth that was already present in John's Gospel.

Here's another example, found in Hebrews 2:9. Did Jesus die "apart from God" (*chōris theou*) or "by God's grace" (*chariti theou*)? Bart Ehrman believes that the author of Hebrews originally wrote *chōris theou*—"apart from God." The manuscript evidence for this wording is weak, but it *is* one possible reading of the text. And yet, either wording fits the larger context of Hebrews. According to Hebrews 13:11-13, Jesus died excluded from the fellowship of God's people. In light of this text—as well as Mark 15:34, which would have been in circulation when Hebrews was written—it would also have made sense to say that Jesus died separated from fellowship with God the Father ("apart from God"). At the same time, according to Hebrews 13:9, it is by God's grace that God's people can endure persecution. So, the more prominent reading—"by God's grace"—also makes sense. Neither possibility contradicts anything in the letter to the Hebrews or in the New Testament as a whole.[6]

THE CASE OF ADDING SCRIPTURE TO SCRIPTURE

Sometimes copyists incorporated other well-known Scriptures into certain biblical texts. Here's a simple example from some scribes who were copying texts that had been expanded in the context of Christian worship: At some point in the late first or early second century, some Christians—probably in Syria—added this paraphrased snippet from 1 Chronicles 29:11 to their recitations of the Lord's Prayer: "For yours is the kingdom and power and glory forever. Amen." Eventually, this addition became so familiar that a copyist included it at the end of Matthew 6:13 when copying his Gospel. Still later, other copyists expanded the version of the Lord's Prayer that's found in Luke 11 to fit the more familiar version in Matthew's Gospel. One text of Scripture was added to another text.

Similarly, in John 19, the author quotes Psalm 22:18 as a prophecy of the soldiers gambling for Jesus' clothing: "This fulfilled the Scripture, 'They parted my clothes among themselves, and upon my clothing they cast lots'" (John 19:24). This quotation eventually worked its way into Matthew's description of the crucifixion (Matthew 27:35). Again, a copyist used one Scripture to expand another Scripture. An annoyance for textual critics and biblical scholars? Somewhat. But are such changes so significant that they alter some aspect of Christian faith? No.

In Luke's description of the baptism of Jesus, a few late manuscripts replace the familiar words from heaven found in other Gospels—"In you, I am well-pleased"—with this quotation from Psalm 2:7: "Today, I have begotten you" (Luke 3:22). Ehrman makes the case that the quotation from the Psalms represents the Gospel's original wording.[7] I don't find Ehrman's case to be compelling at this point.[8] Yet, even if the quotation from the psalms *was* the original wording, both the change and the original wording affirm truths about Jesus Christ that appear throughout the New Testament (see Matthew 3:17; Mark 1:11; Acts 13:33; Hebrews 1:5; 5:5).

In Matthew 27, another example of this sort of alteration appears: In Matthew 27:34, some later manuscripts have "they gave him *vinegar* to drink" in place of "they gave him *wine* to drink." Ehrman portrays this change as a possible attempt to avoid inconsistency between this text and Matthew 26:29, where Jesus says, "I will certainly not drink from this fruit that comes from the vine until that day when I drink it new with you in my Father's kingdom." Though possible, this scenario is quite unlikely. After all, in the first century, vinegar and wine were *both* products of "fruit that comes from the vine."[9] (When Jesus promised not to drink the fruit of the vine again until the consummation of God's kingdom, he was most likely pointing his apostles' attention to the banquet that Jews believed would mark the beginning of the Messiah's reign.[10]) Why, then, did a copyist change the text? Most likely because the copyist remembered a passage from the Psalms that reads, "For my thirst they gave me vinegar" (Psalm 69:21).

Since scribes frequently copied all four New Testament Gospels consecutively, it's not surprising that copyists occasionally changed the wording of one Gospel to fit the others. For example, a few manuscripts of Mark 6:3 have "carpenter's son" in place of "carpenter." Despite Ehrman's attempts to ascribe other intentions to some hapless scribe, it's most probable that the copyist simply adapted Mark 6:3 to match the parallel passage in Matthew 13:55. This change caused some confusion among early Christian theologians, including Origen of Alexandria.[11] But, again, these modifications are easily discovered, and I do not know any cardinal doctrine of Christian faith that depends on whether Jesus was a *carpenter* or a *carpenter's son,* especially in a culture in which sons typically took up the same trade as their fathers.

THE CASE OF COPYISTS WHO KNEW TOO MUCH

In other cases, copyists seem to have felt that the biblical text didn't provide all the information that readers needed. So, copyists supplemented the text not with other Scriptures but with their own knowledge. For example, many late manuscripts add a couple of clauses around John 5:3-4 to explain why so many physically disadvantaged persons had gathered around the pool known as Beth-zatha or Beth-saida:

> They were waiting for the water to move, because an angel from the Lord went down at certain times into the pool and stirred the water; whoever stepped in first after the stirring of the water was healed of any disease.

None of the most ancient Greek manuscripts include these words, although the addition probably *does* preserve a widespread belief about the Pool of Beth-zatha. Otherwise, the paralyzed man's words in John 5:7 wouldn't make any sense: "Lord," the paralytic pleads, "I have no person in order that someone might throw me into the pool when the water is stirred." At some point—perhaps in an area far from Jerusalem, where this odd notion wasn't widely understood—a knowledgeable scribe felt that readers needed an explanation of this custom.

Similarly, a copyist of Mark's Gospel seems to have recognized that the prophetic quotation in the opening verses of the Gospel According to Mark comes not only from Isaiah 40:3 but also from Malachi 3:1 with a partial phrase thrown in from Exodus 23:20. Ehrman depicts this as an error in Mark's Gospel. But Isaiah is the most prominent prophet in the mix, and it was a common practice to cite combined quotations by the most prominent source.[12] Still, some later scribe may have seen a potential problem here, as Ehrman does. As a result, this copyist changed the opening words of Mark 1:2 from "just as it has been written in *Isaiah the prophet*" to "just as it has been written in *the prophets.*"

Other scribal additions of this sort include traditions that were *not* part of the original document but that may still represent authentic accounts of what happened. For example, in some manuscripts of Luke's Gospel, Luke 23:34 is missing. While the omission doesn't call into question any aspect of Christian faith, these words of Jesus from the cross—"Father, forgive them; they do not know what they're doing"—have had a profound effect on many people. Ehrman argues that this verse was originally present in Luke's Gospel but that anti-Jewish Christians cut it out. Even he must admit, though, that the earliest and best manuscripts *don't* include this particular passage. It's far more likely that a later scribe *added* this verse to the Gospel According to Luke.

When it comes to Luke 23:34—as well as several other expansions in the Gospels—it appears that the copyist incorporated a familiar tradition that had already circulated among the churches for several decades. These traditions may have been reliable, but they were not written in the original Gospel manuscripts. Personally, I suspect that Jesus *did* say from the cross, "Father, forgive them; they do not know what they're doing"; these words were simply not present in the first edition of Luke's Gospel.

Two other examples can be found elsewhere in this Gospel, in Luke 22:43-44 and 24:12. In Luke 22:43-44, some later texts describe an angel comforting Jesus as the suffering Messiah's sweat mingles with blood.[13] In Luke 24:12, some manuscripts add a brief account of Simon Peter's experience at the empty tomb—one that seems to draw from the same tradition as John 21:3-10. Reliable traditions? Very possibly. Part of Luke's original Gospel? Probably not.

In this tenth-century minuscule manuscript of Mark's Gospel, known as 669, "as it is written in Isaiah the prophet" has been changed to "as it is written in the prophets" (Mark 1:2). (Photograph courtesy of CSNTM.org.)

There are also some longer examples of these sorts of additions to the New Testament. One of the most famous is the beloved account of the woman caught in adultery (John 7:53–8:11)—a poignant and profound story, to be sure, but not part of John's original Gospel. It's missing completely from early manuscripts such as the third-century papyri $\mathfrak{P}^{66}$ and $\mathfrak{P}^{75}$, as well as the Sinaiticus and Vaticanus codices. Even when this story *does* appear in ancient manuscripts, its location changes. Sometimes it's found after John 7:36; other times it's at the end of John's Gospel. Once, the story even shows up in the Gospel According to *Luke,* and—from the writings of a fourth-century Christian named Eusebius of Caesarea—it seems that the story also appeared in a now-lost Gospel known as *Gospel to the Hebrews.*[14]

Mark 16:9-20 might be another example. The most ancient manuscripts of Mark's Gospel end with this awkward clause: "Nothing to anyone did they say, for they were fearing" (Mark 16:8b). Apparently, this abrupt ending bothered more than one scribe.[15] To this ending, a few texts from the seventh, eighth and ninth centuries A.D. add a pithy postscript:[16]

> All that they were told, they reported briefly to Peter and those around him. After these things, Jesus sent out by means of them, from east to west, the sacred and immortal message of salvation unto the ages.

Other manuscripts add the verses that we know as Mark 16:9-20. Again, these verses probably weren't in Mark's original Gospel, but they *do* represent an authentic tradition about Jesus' resurrection. When this is taken into consideration, it becomes clear—in the words of Bruce Metzger—"that the New Testament contains not four but five evangelic accounts of events subsequent to the Resurrection of Christ."[17]

The verses added to Mark 16 *do* seem at first to include some strange teachings: "They will take hold of snakes, and, if they drink something poisonous, it will not hurt them," the text declares (Mark 16:18a). Unless I miss my guess, these promises were never intended as a divine calling to guzzle cyanide or juggle rattlesnakes. Their intent was to illustrate in picturesque metaphors how God is able to protect his people from any enemy. What's more, both promises are also present in other biblical passages. A reference to protection from

LOOK IT UP

Textual critics have developed several terms to describe the unintentional errors that copyists made as they copied the New Testament documents:

homonymity (from Greek, *homōnymos,* "same name") Textual variant that seems to be the result of mishearing one word as another similar-sounding word.

permutation (from Latin, *permutare,* "to change completely") Textual variant that seems to be the result of faulty eyesight.

parablepsis (from Greek, "looking beside") Textual variant that seems to be the result of a copyist unintentionally omitting or repeating a word or series of words because of a skip of the eye.[18]

dittography (from Greek, *dittos* ["double"] + *graphos* ["writing"]) Incidence of parablepsis that seems to be the result of a copyist copying a word or series of words twice.

haplography (from Greek, *haplos* ["single"] + *graphos* ["writing"]) Incidence of parablepsis that seems to be the result of a copyist skipping a word or series of words.

homoioteleuton or **homoeoteleuton** (from Greek, *homoi* ["like"] + *telos* ["ending"]) Incidence of haplography caused by the copyist's eyes skipping to a later word or phrase that ended in a similar way to the word or phrase that the copyist was reproducing.

homoioarcton or **homoeoarcton** (from Greek, *homoi* ["like"] + *archē* ["beginning"]) Incidence of haplography caused by the copyist's eyes skipping to a later word or phrase that began in a similar way to the word or phrase that the copyist was reproducing.

serpents is found in Luke's Gospel (Luke 10:19; compare Isaiah 11:8), and the promise of protection from poison echoes Psalm 69: "They gave me poison for food, . . . I am lowly and in pain; let your salvation, O God, protect me" (Psalm 69: 21, 29). Again, none of the additions alters Christian faith or practice in any significant way.

4

Truth About "Misquoting Jesus"

*Ehrman makes the provocative case that many of our
cherished biblical stories and widely held beliefs concerning the divinity of Jesus, the Trinity, and the divine
origins of the Bible itself stem from both intentional
and accidental alterations by scribes.*

PROMOTIONAL COVER COPY FROM
MISQUOTING JESUS

Not every intentional change in the New Testament texts is quite
as clear-cut as the ones I've listed so far. There *are* intentional changes
in the manuscripts that could affect the reader's understanding of a
particular text. And still, none of them challenges any vital aspect of
Christian faith.

WHAT DID JESUS KNOW AND WHEN DID HE KNOW IT?

It seems, for example, that Matthew 24:36 originally read, "About
that day and hour, no one knows—neither the angels of the heavens
nor the Son, but only the Father." At some point, a copyist either accidentally skipped a few words in the text—an example of haplo-
graphic parablepsis—or couldn't handle the idea that Jesus *didn't*
know the day or hour of the end of time. As a result, some manu-

scripts leave out the words "nor the Son." If this were the only appearance of this passage, this *could* have some effect on the interpreter's understanding of the precise relationship between Jesus'
divine and human natures. But the words "nor the Son" appear with
no textual variations in the parallel passage in Mark 13:32! Even if an
authentic question *did* exist about this text, no vital aspect of my faith
in Jesus Christ as the risen Lord depends on whether Jesus could
have located the apocalypse on a desk calendar during his time on
this earth.

THE MISSING CLAUSE

Another example of this type of change can be found in the letter
known as 1 John. Here's an English translation of what you would
find in 1 John 5:7-8 in Textus Receptus, a Greek New Testament created by a scholar named Erasmus in the 1500s:

> For there are three who bear witness in heaven: the Father, the
> Word, and the Holy Spirit; and these three are one. And there
> are three that bear witness on earth: the Spirit, the water, and
> the blood; and these three agree as one. (NKJV)

The problem is, the middle portion of this text appears in a Greek
manuscript for the first time in the Renaissance era—and there's
every reason to think that it was a forged addition even in that text![1]
When Erasmus put together the Textus Receptus in the 1500s, he
himself questioned the authenticity of these clauses.

In the overwhelming majority of Greek manuscripts, 1 John 5:7-
8 reads more like this: "For there are three that testify: The Spirit, the
water, and the blood; and these three are one." Ehrman—along with
every other competent biblical scholar who has looked at this text in
the past hundred years—believes that someone expanded this text

KNOW MORE

As textual critics examined the New Testament texts, they noticed
certain similarities that allowed them to group the manuscripts into
three "families." Each family represents a certain pattern of preservation and changes in the New Testament manuscripts. By compar-
ing the families, textual critics are often able to determine *when* and
where certain changes occurred:

1. The *Western* text emerged and circulated primarily in Italy, Gaul
   (modern France) and North Africa. Some important Western wit-
   nesses are the papyri $\mathfrak{P}^{48}$ and $\mathfrak{P}^{38}$, as well as Codex Bezae (D).
   Copyists of the Western texts seem to have paraphrased fre-
   quently and freely added to their manuscripts.

2. Texts from the *Alexandrian* family came from the area around Alexandria, Egypt. Because of the dryness of this area, many of the
   most ancient surviving texts—including $\mathfrak{P}^{66}$, $\mathfrak{P}^{75}$, Codex Sinaiticus and Codex Vaticanus—come from the Alexandrian family.

3. The *Byzantine* text was the dominant text in the eastern part of the
   Roman Empire. Most Greek manuscripts of the New Testament are
   Byzantine texts, so the Byzantine text is also known as the *Majority Text.* Most scholars consider Byzantine manuscripts to be later
   and less reliable than Alexandrian manuscripts. When Erasmus
   collated the Textus Receptus—from which the King James Version was translated—the only texts available to him were Byzantine manuscripts.

more than a thousand years after the letter was written.[2] That's why the only translations that have included the longer version of these verses are renderings that are somehow bound to the Textus Receptus. Still, no Christian doctrine depends on the longer version of 1 John 5:7-8. Matthew 28:19-20 states the concept of one God ("in the *name*," singular) expressed in three persons ("of the Father and of the Son and of the Holy Spirit") just as clearly as these words that someone added to 1 John.

MODIFIED TO OPPOSE WOMEN AND JEWS?

According to Ehrman, this category of alterations also includes changes that occurred because copyists "who were not altogether satisfied with what the New Testament books said modified their words to make them . . . more vigorously oppose heretics, women, Jews, and pagans."[3] Yet, as far as I can tell, he fails to come up with even *one* significant change that can't be corrected by looking carefully at manuscript evidence from the ancient world.

Despite Ehrman's contention that a scribe excised Luke 23:34 because of anti-Jewish sentiments, the manuscripts don't support this supposition, as we have already seen. It does seem that some changes may have been made at various times to shield Christian faith from the charges of pagans and heretics. But we've already looked at many of these changes and discovered no changes that are significant for Christian faith or practice.

A handful of changes *could* potentially relate to the role of women in churches today. It appears that women played more prominent roles in the early church than they did in the later eras. As a result, some scribes in late ancient and medieval times seem to have altered texts that seemed to place women in prominent positions.

For example, in the most ancient manuscripts of Acts 18:26, a woman named Priscilla seems to be the primary teacher of Apollos. Centuries later, a copyist switched the order of names, placing the name of Priscilla's husband, Aquila, first. In Romans 16:7, someone named Junia—a woman's name—is said to be "significant among the apostles," but a later scribe turned "Junia" into "Junias," a man's name.[4] In Acts 17:4, another scribe changed "prominent women" into "wives of prominent men." In each of these cases, however, it's possible to look at the manuscripts and recover the original wording.[5]

Less certain is Ehrman's claim that a later copyist added 1 Corinthians 14:34-35—verses that declare, in the King James Version, "it is a shame for women to speak in the church"—to Paul's original letter. In some Greek manuscripts, these two verses appear after 1 Corinthians 14:33, but other manuscripts place them after 1 Corinthians 14:40. To some scholars, including Ehrman, this suggests that later scribes added these sentences to Paul's text. Three Greek manuscripts *do* place these disputed sentences after verse 40, but *no* surviving text omits the verses completely. *Every* surviving manuscript includes these verses, and all of the earliest and best Greek texts place them after verse 33. Consequently, Ehrman's reconstruction seems less than convincing. Whether or not these words were present in Paul's original epistle, it is possible to understand them in ways that value women as equal partners with men in God's work.[6] Most likely, Paul was simply emphasizing that he expected women to follow the same guidelines as everyone else in being silent while others were teaching and by learning from wiser believers.

Certainly, these verses have been misconstrued at times in ways that dishonor and subjugate women. This is inexcusable—just as Christians' choices to twist the good news of Jesus Christ into excuses to violate Jewish people and to suppress African Americans have been inexcusable. And yet, the fault is not with the biblical text. It is with the choices of individuals to wrench the biblical text to sanction something less than what God has offered humanity in Jesus Christ.

MISQUOTING JESUS OR MISQUOTING TRUTH?

Before leaving the issue of the textual integrity of the New Testament, I want to take a closer look at three specific texts. These are passages that—from Ehrman's perspective—scribes have changed in ways that are so "highly significant" that they alter our understanding of entire books of the Bible.

Mark 1:41-43: Angry, Compassionate or Both? Most translations of Mark 1:41-42 describe Jesus' healing of a skin-diseased man something like this: "Feeling compassion and stretching out his hand, he touched him and said, 'I want to.' Immediately, the skin disease fled from the man, and he was cleansed."

So what's the difficulty? Ehrman believes that the text should *not* read "feeling compassion" (Greek, *splanchnistheis*);[7] in his estimation, the original reading of the text was "becoming angry" (Greek, *orgistheis*). Ehrman goes so far as to imply that this reading affects "the interpretation of an entire book of the New Testament."[8]

Although the manuscript evidence for "becoming angry" *is* mixed, I find Ehrman's case for *orgistheis* to be convincing.[9] It makes far more sense to think that a copyist changed "becoming angry" to "feeling compassion" than for the opposite to have occurred. And, in Greek, the two words neither look alike nor sound alike, so this can't be an issue of confusing similar terms.[10]

Still, I fail to see how (in Ehrman's estimation) this single word changes our understanding of Jesus or of Mark's Gospel. With or without *orgistheis* in Mark 1:41, this Gospel depicts Jesus as a passionate prophet,[11] rapidly crisscrossing Galilee and Judea as he moves toward his impending encounter with a Roman cross. By the third chapter, Jesus has already upset so many religious leaders that they're making plans to murder him (Mark 3:6). He becomes annoyed when people don't trust him (Mark 3:5; 9:23). At the same time, Mark makes it clear that Jesus constantly feels compassion for downtrodden people (Mark 6:34; 8:2; 9:22-23). Based on evidence throughout this Gospel, either reading of the text would fit Mark's presentation of Jesus. Understanding the text to declare that Jesus became angry does not significantly change my understanding of Mark's Gospel.

Ehrman *does* err at one point in his analysis of this text, though. Ehrman claims that, after Jesus heals the man,

> he "severely rebukes him" and "throws him out" [Mark 1:43]. These are literal renderings of the Greek words, which are usually softened in translation. They are harsh terms, used elsewhere in Mark always in the contexts of violent conflict and aggression.[12]

Although *ekballō*—the term Ehrman translates "throws him out"—does sometimes appear in Mark's Gospel in the context of violent conflict, the term does *not* "always" function in this sense. In Mark 5:40, *ekballō* describes how Jesus sent a deceased child's family from the room where her body lay. I don't think Mark intended us to envision Jesus grabbing the girl's parents by the collar and hurling them through the door. It's *possible* that *ekballō* carries such a meaning in Mark 1:12—"the Spirit violently hurled Jesus out into the desert"—but it's more likely that Mark simply intended *ekballō* to convey the vibrant urgency that makes this Gospel so fascinating.

So what actually happened when Jesus healed this leprous man? And, if Jesus was angry, *why* was he angry? It's important to notice *where* Jesus was teaching when this healing occurred. Apparently Jesus was in a synagogue (Mark 1:39) where the Jews of the town had gathered to hear God's Word. If so, this man's presence could have rendered an entire Jewish community unclean! Although Jesus challenged the traditions that had been *added* to the Law of Moses, he consistently called his people to live by the laws that God had graciously given them through Moses (see Mark 1:44). According to these laws, the leprous man was *supposed* to have sequestered himself away from his fellow Jews (Leviticus 13). Instead, he placed an entire Jewish community in danger of ceremonial uncleanness. Is it any wonder that Jesus became angry? And still, *Jesus healed him.*

So was Jesus *angry* or was he *compassionate?*

Yes.[13]

Luke 22:19-20 and Luke 22:43-44: Why Did Jesus Die? When it comes to Luke 22, Ehrman argues that a later scribe added Luke 22:19-20—and he may be correct. Solid evidence *does* exist to suggest that these specific verses may not have appeared in the first edi-

---

And he took bread, gave thanks and broke it, and gave it to them, saying, "This is my body given for you; do this in remembrance of me."

In the same way, after the supper he took the cup, saying, "This cup is the new covenant in my blood, which is poured out for you."

Luke 22:19-20 NIV

---

tion of Luke's Gospel. Various forms of these same sentences *do* appear, however, in Matthew 26:27-28, Mark 14:22-25 and 1 Corinthians 11:23-25. So, even if these clauses were missing from Luke's original writing, this is not a case of "misquoting Jesus"—it's a passage that was already present in several other places, though perhaps not in Luke's Gospel.

Ehrman proposes the absence of these verses as proof that the author of Luke's Gospel didn't view Jesus' death in quite the same way as the authors of the other Gospels.

> Luke . . . has a different understanding of the way in which Jesus' death leads to salvation than does Mark (and Paul, and other early Christian writers). . . . It is not that Jesus' death is unimportant. It is *extremely* important for Luke—but not as an atonement. Instead, Jesus' death is what makes people realize their guilt before God.[14]

So, from Ehrman's perspective, although Luke used Mark's Gospel and perhaps Paul's letters as sources—a logical assumption based on Luke 1:1-3—Luke changed wordings that might suggest Jesus died for people's sins. Later copyists, Ehrman claims, added Luke 22:19-20 to emphasize the flesh-and-blood humanity of Jesus. (Though I'm open to his point that later copyists added these two verses, Ehrman's rationale for the change is quite unlikely. The physical body of Jesus is already emphasized in Luke 24:24-43, not to mention in Luke's narratives of Jesus' birth and childhood. It's more likely that copyists included these verses because they had become familiar in the context of Christian worship, much like the additions to the Lord's Prayer that we discussed earlier.)

So did Luke really disagree with Mark and Paul and other writers about the death of Jesus?

Ehrman is correct that Luke's Gospel doesn't emphasize Jesus' death as an atoning sacrifice for people's sins. The idea of sacrificial atonement for sins was, after all, more prominent in *Jewish* theology, and Luke was writing for an audience that was more influenced by Greek culture. For this audience, what was most meaningful wasn't that Jesus would suffer as a sacrifice for sin. What would impress them was the fact that a person so righteous and so divine would submit himself not only to live in human flesh but also to die the darkest possible death.[15]

This does *not* mean, however, that Luke did not view Jesus' death in terms of atonement. Neither does it mean that the sacrificial aspect of the crucifixion didn't interest Luke. It simply means that sacrificial atonement was not the aspect of Jesus' death that was most meaningful to Luke's audience. So, Luke focused on Jesus as a divine martyr—a *different* emphasis, to be sure, but not at odds with other New Testament depictions of Jesus. Simply put, different emphases do not amount to contradictory understandings of the same event.

The same point may be made when it comes to Luke 22:43-44. Here, some unknown copyist added a couple of clauses to emphasize Jesus' passionate prayer in Gethsemane. Ehrman argues that only in these verses did Luke portray Jesus in dread or distress:

> Rather than entering his passion with fear and trembling, in anguish over his coming fate, the Jesus of Luke goes to his death calm and in control. . . . It is clear that Luke does not share Mark's understanding that Jesus was in anguish, bordering on despair.[16]

It's true that Luke's Gospel doesn't emphasize the dread Jesus seems to have felt in the Garden of Gethsemane. But did Luke actually "not share Mark's understanding" of Jesus' suffering, or did Luke simply highlight a different aspect of Jesus' death? It's true that Luke's focus changed because he was addressing a different audience. But, once again, different emphases do not amount to contradictory understandings of the same event.

WHO WAS REALLY MISQUOTED?

The promotional copy for *Misquoting Jesus* claims that "many of our cherished biblical stories and widely held beliefs concerning the divinity of Jesus, the Trinity, and the divine origins of the Bible itself stem from both intentional and accidental alterations by scribes." And, supposedly, Ehrman makes this case "for the first time."[17]

As I examine *Misquoting Jesus,* I find nothing that measures up to the title or to the promotional copy. What I find is a great deal of discussion about a handful of textual variants—none of which ultimately changes any essential belief that's presented in the New Testament. What's more, despite the sensational title of *Misquoting Jesus,* I find only a half-dozen times when Jesus *might* have been misquoted, and most of these supposed changes simply echo ideas that are found elsewhere in Scripture.

And, so, returning to our initial questions: Have the New Testament manuscripts changed over the centuries? Without a doubt! But are the changes in the manuscripts "highly significant"? And do any of them "affect the interpretation of an entire book of the New Testament"? Not that I can tell.

WHY THE LOST CHRISTIANITIES
WERE LOST

What was lost in the first few centuries of Christianity wasn't only the earliest manuscripts of the New Testament, according to Ehrman. There were alternative forms of Christian faith that were lost too. According to Ehrman, in the church's first three centuries,

> there was no agreed-upon canon—and no agreed-upon theology. Instead, there was a wide range of diversity: diverse groups asserting diverse theologies based on diverse written texts, all claiming to be written by apostles of Jesus.[1]

This diversity wasn't simply a matter of denominational labels or disagreement over styles of worship. There were *Ebionites,* who viewed Jesus as a human prophet, and *Gnostics,* who believed Jesus was somehow divine but that he only *seemed* human. Then, there were the folk to whom Ehrman refers as *proto-orthodox*—Christians with beliefs similar to the ones we find in our New Testaments today. By the mid-second century, the followers of a man named Marcion had become part of the mix too.[2] Each group had Scriptures that claimed to be apostolic. Yet, from Ehrman's perspective, none of these texts—including the ones that found their way into the New

Testament—represented reliable, eyewitness testimony about Jesus.[3]

What's more, according to Ehrman, the precise contents of what we call Christian faith didn't emerge primarily from reflection on the historical person of Jesus or on the writings of eyewitnesses of his ministry. What determined the final shape of Christian faith was primarily the struggle between these various factions:

> As soon as some of Jesus' followers pronounced their belief that he had been raised from the dead, Christians [of every type] began to understand that Jesus himself was, in some way, the only means of a right standing before God, the only way of salvation. But once that happened, a new factor entered the religious scene of antiquity. Christians by their very nature became exclusivists, claiming to be right in such a way that everyone else was necessarily wrong. . . . Belief had to be in *something,* rather than some kind of vague, abstract faith that things were right (or wrong) with the world, then Christians, with their exclusive claims, had to decide what the content of faith was to be.[4]

Once the "proto-orthodox Christians" triumphed, they rewrote the historical record.[5]

> Virtually all forms of modern Christianity, . . . go back to *one* form of Christianity that emerged as victorious from the conflicts of the second and third centuries. . . . This victorious party rewrote the history of the controversy, making it appear that there had not been much of a conflict at all, claiming that its own views had always been those of the majority of Christians at all times, back to the time of Jesus and his apostles, that its perspective, in effect, had always been "orthodox" (i.e., the "right belief").[6]

A glance at the New Testament reveals that Ehrman is partly correct. There *were* many divergent sets of beliefs that circulated in the churches—all of them most likely claiming to be Christian. Some people rejected the possibility of a physical resurrection (1 Corinthians 15). Others believed that keeping the law of Moses was a necessary outward expression of Christian faith (Acts 15). Still others denied that Jesus was a physical being at all (1 John 4:1-3). And these controversies didn't end with the deaths of the apostles! In fact, as each set of beliefs developed in the second and third centuries, the divisions grew deeper.

Twelfth-century copy of Origen of Alexandria's homilies on Genesis and Exodus. In his messages on Genesis, Origen spoke strongly against the Gnostic understanding of God's creation. (Photograph of MS021 courtesy of The Schøyen Collection, Oslo and London.)

But the crucial question isn't, Were there serious struggles for several centuries among people who claimed to be Christians? There *were*. The question is, Which understanding of Jesus represents authentic, historical testimony about him? I happen to believe that the New Testament preserves precisely this sort of testimony.

Ehrman's own rule of thumb in determining historical truth is that, "particularly in the ancient world, . . . earlier is better."[7] In other words, the sources closest to the original event are most likely to be correct—especially if those sources represent eyewitness accounts.

What I find as I look at the available evidence is that the New Testament bears every mark of containing ancient, reliable, eyewitness testimonies about Jesus.

Even if you don't agree with what I'm saying, take an open-minded look with me at the New Testament and ask yourself what you see. Consider the cultural and historical contexts of these writings and, at some point before our journey ends, ask yourself, What are the chances that these documents are true? And, if they *are* true, what does that mean for my life?

5

TRUTH ABOUT ORAL HISTORY

Sometimes Christian apologists say there are only three options to who Jesus was: a liar, a lunatic, or the Lord. But there could be a fourth option—legend.

BART D. EHRMAN

Chances are, if you really want to remember something today, you will scribble it in a notebook or in the palm of your hand or on the knee of your blue jeans. You might even scrawl it in the inside cover of this book. (It's okay if you do; really, it is.) That's because you live in a culture that relies on written words—even when it comes to small items like shopping lists, telephone numbers and the ever-growing catalog of items that your spouse wants you to do around the house.[1]

Suppose that, sometime this week, several witnesses claimed simultaneously that a condemned criminal came back to life three days after drawing his last breath in an electric chair. Since you and I live in a culture that's centered on printed pictures and words, the story would race in written form through newspapers and blogs and tabloids in a matter of hours. Within a few weeks, the story of the converted IRS agent named Matthew would show up in *The Wall Street Journal*, a half-dozen fishing magazines would be offering exclusive interviews with Simon and Andrew, and the editors of *People* would drop their planned cover story about the latest celebrity baby to feature the secret anguish of Judas Iscariot, complete with never-before-seen photographs from the scene of his demise. Simply put, printed records define our culture.

Not so in the first century.

In the world of Jesus and Mary and Simon Peter, *written records were secondary to spoken narratives*. So, when the Gospels were first written, people were more likely to *memorize* what happened than to write it down. "For my own part," one ancient orator commented, "I think we should not write anything which we do not intend to commit to memory."[2] According to the philosopher Plato,

---

THINK IT OUT

At the end of the first century A.D., some Christian leaders still relied on oral accounts of Jesus' life alongside the written Gospels and apostolic epistles. Papias of Hierapolis put it this way: "If anyone who had served the elders came, I asked about their sayings in detail— what, according to the elders, Andrew or Peter said, or what was said by Philip or Thomas or James or John or Matthew or any other of the Lord's followers. . . . For I perceived that what was to be obtained from books would not profit me as much as what came from the living and surviving voice."[3]

---

persons should record their thoughts in written form only "to treasure up reminders for [themselves] when [they] come to the forgetfulness of old age."[4]

This cultural tendency existed partly because so few people knew *how* to write and read in the first century A.D.[5] It existed also because the character of the person spreading a story mattered so deeply to ancient people. (In some cases, first-century folk may have been *less likely* to trust written records, because they couldn't speak personally with the individual that was telling the story!)[6] As a result, truths were often preserved in the form of *oral history*.[7] To be sure, not every story that circulated in the ancient world qualified as oral history, and there may be some instances when such histories become inconsistent. The point here is simply that, in the cultural context of the first century, oral history provided a primary pathway for reliable preservation of past truths.[8]

JESUS, A LEGEND?

In such a context, it shouldn't surprise anyone that three decades may have passed between the moment when Mary Magdalene first claimed she saw Jesus alive and the time that the first Gospel was

---

FACT SHEET

When were the New Testament Gospels probably written? Here are the dates that most scholars—including Bart Ehrman—assign to the Gospels:

- *The Gospel According to Matthew:* Between 75 and 85, though many scholars believe that an Aramaic forerunner of this Gospel was in circulation in the 60s or earlier
- *The Gospel According to Mark:* Between 65 and 70
- *The Gospel According to Luke:* Between 65 and 85
- *The Gospel According to John:* Between 75 and 95

---

written. What's more, this shouldn't cause anyone to question the re-liability of the Gospels—especially if it's possible to show that a consistent oral history of the key events of Jesus' life existed among the earliest witnesses of his resurrection.

Ehrman seems, however, to view the gap between the earthly ministry of Jesus and the writing of the Gospels as a serious problem. Here's what Ehrman has stated about this gap:

> [The New Testament Gospels] were written thirty-five to sixty-five years after Jesus' death, . . . not by people who were eyewitnesses, but by people living later. . . . Where did these people get their information from? . . . After the days of Jesus, people started telling stories about him in order to convert others to the faith. . . . Stories are in circulation year after year after year, and as a result of that, the stories get changed.[9]

It's on this basis that Ehrman repeatedly claims in interviews and lectures: "Sometimes Christian apologists say there are only three options to who Jesus was: a liar, a lunatic, or the Lord. But there could be a fourth option—legend."[10] This fourth option is the one that, from Ehrman's perspective, best fits the historical evidence.

So, what if he's right?

What if the description of Jesus in the New Testament Gospels isn't historically accurate? What if no one knows who actually wrote the New Testament Gospels? What if the story of Jesus' resurrection is simply the result of a series of legends that changed over time? And what if these Gospels aren't even based on eyewitness accounts in the first place? If so, Ehrman might be completely correct when he calls Christian faith a "dead end."

Despite Ehrman's apparent confidence about his conclusions, I'm convinced that there are some difficulties in his interpretation of the data. The historical reliability of the New Testament Gospels can't be discounted nearly as easily as he implies. With this in mind, let's wrestle a difficult question that forms the foundation of Ehrman's claims: Did the stories about Jesus change significantly as they circulated year after year? In the next chapter, we'll look at a second question: Were the original New Testament Gospels actually anonymous documents?

DID THE STORY STAY THE SAME?

Have you ever played Telephone? You know, the game in which one person whispers a sentence to someone else, that person whispers what she or he hears to the next person in the circle, and so on? At the end, the first person and the last person reveal their sentences, and everyone laughs at how much the sentence changed between the first and last communicators.

I last remember playing this game in the fourth grade when my teacher was trying to occupy an unruly class on a rainy day. I did not want to play Telephone; I wanted to do something constructive, such as painting my ruler like a lightsaber and smacking fellow students with it—a pastime for which Mrs. Redwing did not share my passion. So, each time a sentence reached me, I changed it completely. The student beside me might say, "The sky is dark and gray today"—but what I would whisper to the next student was something like, "Mrs. Redwing's hair looks like a mangy Wookiee's armpit." For some reason, I found this to be considerably more amusing than my teacher did; I think she was just jealous because *her* ruler wasn't painted like a lightsaber.

Despite my distaste for the game, I did pick up this truth from playing Telephone: Even without an obstinate nine-year-old in the circle, it's possible for a statement to change dramatically whenever it's passed from one person to another. According to Ehrman, this is precisely what happened to the earliest stories about Jesus:

> Stories based on eyewitness accounts are not necessarily reliable, and the same is true a hundredfold for accounts that— even if stemming from reports of eyewitnesses—have been in oral circulation long after the fact. . . . Imagine playing "Telephone" not in a solitary living room with ten kids on a sunny afternoon in July, but over the expanse of the Roman Empire (some 2,500 miles across!) with thousands of participants from different backgrounds, with different concerns, and in different contexts, some of whom have to translate the stories into different languages all over the course of decades. What would happen to the stories?[11]

"What would happen"—according to Ehrman—is that these stories would end up radically changed. "Stories were changed with what would strike us today as reckless abandon," Ehrman claims. "They were modified, amplified, and embellished. And sometimes they were made up."[12] In other words, from Ehrman's perspective, the earliest Christians passed on their traditions in much the same way as I played Telephone as a nine-year-old. And, according to Ehrman, the first clear tradition of Jesus' resurrection came "well over twenty *years*" after Jesus died.[13] If Ehrman is right, the New Testament Gospels are the befuddled results of more than two decades of people inventing and embellishing stories about Jesus.

But are Ehrman's claims true? Did the earliest Christians actually change stories with "reckless abandon"? And did two decades really pass before any clear tradition about Jesus' resurrection emerged? As it turns out, historical evidence from the first century A.D. simply doesn't support Ehrman's reconstruction.

How First-Century Oral History Functioned

In the first place, Ehrman seems unwilling to recognize the vast difference between how oral history would fare in *today's* world and how accurately people in the ancient world might have preserved the same tradition. People in today's technologized world—surrounded by high levels of literacy and easy access to writing materials—are accustomed to recording important information in written form. So, you and I probably *would* have a tough time maintaining consistent, reliable oral history for more than a few months.

Not so in the ancient world.

Especially among the Jews, important teachings were told and retold in rhythmic, repetitive patterns so that students could memorize key truths.[14] As a result, it was possible for a rabbi's oral teachings to remain amazingly consistent from one generation to the next.[15] Here's how a Jewish philosopher named Philo described this sort of process: "[The leader's] instruction proceeds in a leisurely manner; he

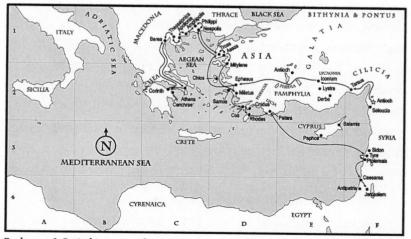

Paul wrote 1 Corinthians around A.D. 53, near the beginning of his third missionary journey. (Map from the *Rose Book of Bible Charts, Maps, and Time Lines.*)

lingers over it and spins it out with repetitions, thus permanently imprinting the thoughts in the souls of the hearers."[16]

These rabbinic patterns of rhythm and repetition are present throughout Jesus' teachings. Think, for example, about how the word *blessed* begins each line of the Beatitudes and how Jesus repeats the phrases "you have heard it said" and "but I say to you" in the Sermon on the Mount (Matthew 5:1-7, 21-47). Such patterns are distinct features of ancient oral traditions.

What's more, there is evidence that it wasn't only Jesus' *teachings* that circulated orally. It seems that brief summaries of the essential events of Jesus' life, death and resurrection circulated in the same way. Let's look at one example of how oral histories were passed from one group of Christians to another. A short time after Jesus died on the cross, a consistent oral account of the crucifixion and resurrection of Jesus emerged—apparently from eyewitnesses of these events![17]

So, where can you find this oral history?

It's found in the New Testament, in the writings of Paul. While dealing with some theological controversies in the city of Corinth, the apostle Paul recalled and recorded an oral account of Jesus' resurrection. Paul's primary purpose in preserving these words was to remind the Corinthians of the truths that he had proclaimed among them three years earlier, around A.D. 50. Yet there are clues in Paul's words that show how quickly an oral account of Jesus' resurrection emerged among his first followers and how consistent the tradition remained as it circulated. Here's what Paul said to the Corinthians:

> For I handed over to you what I also received:
> That the Messiah died on behalf of our sins according to the
> Scriptures,

And that he was buried,
And that he rose on the third day according to the Scriptures,
And that he was seen by Cephas,
then the Twelve;
then, he was seen
by more than five hundred brothers at once; . . .
then, he was seen by James,
then by all the apostles.
(1 Corinthians 15:3-7)[18]

So, how can scholars know that these words actually came from an early oral history? In the first place, Paul introduced this summation with two Greek words that clearly indicated it was oral tradition. These two words were *paradidōmi* ("handed over" in my translation above) and *paralambanō* ("received"). Ancient readers understood these two words—when used together—to imply that the writer was quoting words that he ~~or she~~ intended to become oral tradition.[19] In this way, Paul clearly informed the Corinthians that he was about to pass on oral tradition.[20]

There are also clues in the text that suggest *where* and *when* the tradition began. Even though Paul was writing in the Greek language to Greek people, he calls Simon Peter by his Aramaic name, *Cephas*. Then, there's the repeated phrase "and that"—a repetition that seems

---

THINK IT OUT

Look carefully at the oral tradition that's preserved in 1 Corinthians 15:3-7. How many essential, theological truths about Jesus are packed into these few poetic lines?

odd unless you're familiar with Hebrew or Aramaic. The phrase rendered "and that" is the Greek translation of a familiar Hebrew and Aramaic method for joining clauses.[21] Based on the vocabulary and grammatical patterns in these verses, it seems that this tradition originally circulated in the Aramaic language.

And where did people primarily speak Aramaic? In Galilee and Judea, the places where Jesus walked and talked, died and ~~allegedly~~ rose from the dead!

And when could Paul possibly have received an oral account of the death and resurrection of Jesus in the Aramaic language? Most likely, Paul learned this tradition around A.D. 35 when he visited the city of Jerusalem.

According to his letter to the Galatians, Paul "went up to Jerusalem to interview Cephas" three years after his experience on the road to Damascus (Galatians 1:18).[22] The Greek term translated "to visit" or "to interview" in Galatians 1:18 is *historeō,* a word that often implied a personal investigation for the purpose of determining historical facts.[23] So, it appears that Paul traveled to Jerusalem to speak with Simon Peter specifically because he wanted to receive the oral history from an eyewitness of the events.[24]

HOW THE STORY STAYED THE SAME

For Paul to have received a consistent oral history in Aramaic no later than A.D. 35, scholars estimate that the tradition must have first surfaced around Jerusalem no later than 32 or 33, perhaps earlier.[25] In other words, a fixed tradition emerged less than thirty-six months after Jesus' crucifixion, near the place of his death, at a time when Jesus' first followers and family members were still living![26]

Perhaps most important, it's obvious that the earliest Christians did *not* recklessly change these traditions. Otherwise, how could

FACT SHEET

- 28-30: Approximate dates of Jesus' earthly ministry, beginning in the fifteenth year of Caesar Tiberius (Luke 3:1).

- 33: Paul sees Jesus on the road to Damascus (Acts 9).

- 33-35: Paul lives in Arabia (Galatians 1:17).

- 35-47: Paul travels to Damascus, Jerusalem and Tarsus (Acts 9–12).

- 47-49: Paul goes to Asia Minor on his first missionary journey. In A.D. 49, Caesar Claudius expels all Jews from Rome—according to Roman historian Suetonius—because of riots "on account of a certain Chrestus," probably a reference to Jesus Christ (Acts 13–15).

- 49-53: Paul embarks on his second missionary journey, establishing a church in Corinth around A.D. 50 (Acts 16–18).

- 53-57: Paul travels to Ephesus on his third missionary journey (Acts 18–21). During this time, Claudius Caesar dies, and Jews return to Rome.

- 57-62: Paul is arrested in Jerusalem, spends two years in Roman custody before appealing to Caesar, then waits two years for Nero Caesar to hear his appeal (Acts 21–28).

- 62-66: Paul may have been released following his appeal, perhaps traveling west of the Italian province. Passing through Rome, Paul may have been arrested and executed—along with Simon Peter—in the aftermath of the fire in Rome.

- 66-70: After years of enduring antagonism from Roman governors, the Jews revolt. Their rebellion culminates in the destruction of the Jewish temple in A.D. 70.

Paul—writing three years after he first visited Corinth—have said to the Corinthians immediately before he quoted this oral history, "I am reminding you, brothers, about the good proclamation that I proclaimed to you" (1 Corinthians 15:1)? For Paul to have made such a statement, he must have proclaimed a similar tradition in each place that he visited. And there's every reason to believe that this same tradition was the one that Paul heard in Jerusalem, only months after Jesus' death.

So, is Ehrman correct when he implies that the earliest Christians changed the stories of Jesus with "reckless abandon"? And did two decades really pass before any clear tradition about Jesus' resurrection emerged, as Ehrman implies?

As far as I can tell, the historical evidence suggests the precise opposite: Within months of Jesus' death, a consistent oral account of Jesus' resurrection emerged among his followers. What's more, this tradition did *not* change from person to person, like a game of Telephone gone terribly wrong. To the contrary, the tradition remained relatively unchanged throughout the first two decades of Christian faith.

Certainly, there were times when *the focus* of certain stories about Jesus changed from one context to another; the different New Testament authors, for example, refined and remolded certain traditions to emphasize their relevance for certain audiences.[27] Yet *the crucial facts* of these stories remained remarkably consistent as they spread year after year across hundreds of cultures and social contexts.[28]

6

TRUTH ABOUT THE
AUTHORS OF THE GOSPELS

*We know that the original manuscripts of the Gospels
did not have their authors' names attached to them.
. . . Christians started attaching names to the various
books that were originally anonymous.*

BART D. EHRMAN

When you glance at the table of contents in your New Testament,
the first four listings on the page are most likely the Gospel According
to Matthew, the Gospel According to Mark, the Gospel According to
Luke and the Gospel According to John. (If the first book in your list
is Acts of the Apostles, turn back a page or two—you've located the
alphabetical index. If the first book in your list is Genesis, you're
looking at the wrong testament! If you see a line that declares, "Persons attempting to find a motive in this narrative will be prosecuted,"
you've picked up the wrong book—you're gaining your spiritual in-
sights from *The Adventures of Huckleberry Finn.*) Based on these traditional ascriptions, most readers assume that four persons named
Matthew, Mark, Luke and John authored the New Testament Gospels. If these four individuals *did* write the Gospels that bear their
names, it may be possible to trace each Gospel to an eyewitness of

Jesus or to persons that had access to eyewitnesses of Jesus.

But what if no one knows who wrote the Gospels? Suppose that four people named Matthew, Mark, Luke and John had nothing to do with the creation of these documents. What if the only reason these names are attached to these writings is that, long after the books were written, some church leaders ascribed these four names to the Gospels?

From what I find in Ehrman's writings, that's precisely what Ehrman wants his readers to believe. Here's what Ehrman has written about the origins of these four names:

> The titles of the Gospels were not put there by their authors—as should be clear after just a moment's reflection. Suppose a disciple named Matthew actually *did* write a book about Jesus' words and deeds. Would he have called it "The Gospel According to Matthew"? Of course not. He might have called it "The Gospel of Jesus Christ" or "The Life and Death of Our Savior" or something similar. But if someone calls it the Gospel *according to Matthew,* then it's obviously someone else trying to explain, at the outset, whose version of the story this one is. And in fact we know that the original manuscripts of the Gospels did not have their authors' names attached to them.[1]
>
> Why then do we call them Matthew, Mark, Luke, and John? Because sometime in the second century, when proto-orthodox Christians recognized the need for *apostolic* authorities, they attributed these books to apostles (Matthew and John) and close companions of apostles (Mark, the secretary of Peter; and Luke the traveling companion of Paul).[2]
>
> Scholars continue to call these books Matthew, Mark, Luke, and John as a matter of convenience; they have to be called

something, and it doesn't make much sense to call them George, Jim, Fred, and Sam.[3]

As proof of his hypothesis, Ehrman makes a point that's technically true: "A wide variety of (different) titles" for the Gospels can be found in ancient manuscripts. According to Ehrman, this fact proves that Christians added the titles later in different times and places.[4]

Now, it's important to point out that the historical accuracy of the New Testament Gospels does *not* depend on determining who penned these documents in the first place. Most scholars would even admit

---

LOOK IT UP

proto-orthodox (from *prōtos* ["before"] and *orthodoxos* ["right belief"]) According to Ehrman, there were no distinct beliefs about Jesus on which all Christians agreed in the first, second and third centuries. There were different, competing opinions from several sects. Ehrman uses the term *proto-orthodox* to describe early Christians whose beliefs were similar to the beliefs that became known as orthodox beliefs later.

---

that it's impossible to prove beyond any doubt who authored the Gospels. At the same time, it *is* possible to demonstrate—based on the available historical records—that some possibilities are *more probable* than others. With that in mind, let's look at the evidence together and consider who may have written the New Testament Gospels!

WHAT THE TITLES TELL US

In the first place, Ehrman isn't quite correct when he claims that, if "a disciple named Matthew actually *did* write a book about Jesus' words and deeds,"[5] the author wouldn't have included his name in the title. In fact, one common pattern for titling books in the ancient world was to place the author's name first, followed by a brief description of the book's contents.[6] For example, the title of Flavius Josephus's history of the Jewish wars was *Flavius Josephus, Historical Investigation of Jewish Conflict,* and his defense of his Jewish heritage began with the ascription "Flavius Josephus, Regarding the Antiquity of the Jews." Similar patterns can be found in the writings of other ancient authors, including Herodotus, Polybius and Plutarch.

So, it's a bit of an overstatement to claim—as Ehrman does—that "in fact we know that the original manuscripts of the Gospels did not have their authors' names attached to them."[7] The truth is, we *don't* know for certain if they did or didn't. When titles *were* attached to ancient books, they often took the form of tags, sewn to the edges of documents. Over the centuries, these tags could have been lost.[8] Still, it's very possible that the first manuscripts of the New Testament Gospels did not have the authors' names included with them. After all— as Ehrman correctly points out—various manuscripts of the New Testament *do* ascribe different names to the Gospels.

For example, in the second-century papyrus $\mathfrak{P}^{64}$ and in two fifth-century codices known as Codex Bezae and Codex Washingtonianus, the title of the first New Testament Gospel is "Gospel According to Matthew." A few early medieval manuscripts have expanded this title to "Holy Gospel According to Matthew" or even "Divine Beginning of the Gospel According to Matthew," while two codices from the fourth century A.D.—Codex Sinaiticus and Codex Vaticanus—begin with the simple title "According to Matthew." And variations of this sort aren't limited to the Gospel According to Matthew![9] The same patterns can be found in the manuscripts of the other three New Testament Gospels too.

So, *why* are there so many variations in the titles of the Gospels? To understand why, imagine with me for a few moments:[10] Suppose that you were a Christian in Rome near the end of the first century, during the reign of Emperor Domitian. Imagine that your congregation had, for several years, read the stories of Jesus from a papyrus codex that people today would recognize as the Gospel According to Mark.

Now, suppose that a trusted member of your congregation returned from a business trip to Ephesus with another account of Jesus' life, one that began with these words: "In the beginning was the Word, and the Word was with God, and the Word was God" (John 1:1). Suddenly, your congregation would need some way to distinguish one Gospel from another. After all, listening to a pastor announce that today's message would come from "That-One-Gospel-that-Begins-with-the-Words-'In-the-Beginning-Was-the-Word'-and-Ends-with-the-Disciples-Catching-153-Fish" would get *really* tiresome after a few weeks. Wouldn't *you* be ready to hear the title shortened to something more manageable, like "According to John"?

TAKING A SECOND LOOK AT THE TITLES

Some scenario of this sort is very possibly how the Gospels ended up with their titles. And, since these titles were ascribed to the Gospels in different times and places, differences in the names of the Gospels developed from place to place.

Does this mean, then, that Ehrman is correct when he claims that the names ascribed to the Gospels have nothing to do with the original authors? Is it true that "sometime in the second century, when proto-orthodox Christians recognized the need for *apostolic* authorities, they attributed these books to apostles . . . and close companions of apostles"?[11]

If that's what's going through your mind at this moment, please take a second look at the different titles that I listed earlier for the Gospel According to Matthew. It's easy to notice how each one is *different*. This time, though, look carefully at what *remains the same* in each title.

What did you notice as you looked at the titles?

Despite the many variations, *every title that's ascribed to this Gospel identifies Matthew as the source*. And this happens not only with the Gospel According to Matthew but also with the other New Testament Gospels. Although the titles vary from place to place, every titled manuscript of the Gospel According to Mark identifies Mark as the Gospel's author—and the same pattern also marks manuscripts of the Gospel According to Luke and the Gospel According to John.

Simply put, what changes from one Gospel manuscript to another is the *precise form* of the title. The identification of the author, however, *never* varies in any New Testament fragment or manuscript that has its title intact. And this unity in titles isn't limited to one region of the Roman Empire—examples of this unity may be found in manuscripts from the western portions of the ancient empire all the way to North Africa, Egypt and Asia Minor.[12]

Why is this consistency so significant?

Think of it this way for a moment: What if the publisher of the book that you're holding right now didn't include *my* name anywhere in the book? Now, imagine that, to distinguish this book from other similar works, the readers of this book had to come up with a probable author. What are the chances that *every group of readers* would ascribe this book to the same author?

Some people might guess that the author was a scholar who had written about the historical blunders in *The Da Vinci Code*—but that grouping would cover dozens of people, including not only me but also Ehrman himself! If someone wanted the book to seem especially authoritative, that person might claim Billy Graham or the pope as the author, however unlikely those ascriptions might be. And, most likely, only a few people in my family would guess that I wrote this book. (Writing this paragraph is *not* improving my self-esteem, by the way.)

Now, add the factors that were present in the Roman Empire—no telephones or email to allow instant communication, and a postal service that took months to transport a letter across the empire. Plus, in the first and second centuries, there was no centrally recognized authority among Christians to force congregations to connect a certain name to each Gospel—no executive director, no denominational board, no international convention of Christians.[13]

Given these factors, what would have happened if different second-century Christian congregations had simply ascribed apostolic names to each Gospel to make these anonymous writings *seem* authoritative, as Ehrman suggests? (Remember, by the second century A.D. the New Testament Gospels had already spread throughout the ancient Roman Empire, far beyond Judea and Rome.[14]) Most likely, each church would have connected a different author with each Gospel. Churches in Asia Minor might have ascribed a Gospel to the apostle Andrew, for example, while churches in Judea might have connected the same Gospel with Thaddeus or James or Jude.

But what would be the likelihood that every group of Christians in the Roman Empire would come up with Mark's name to describe the shortest Gospel or that everyone would name Matthew as the author of the Gospel that begins with a genealogy? And what's the probability of every church in the Roman Empire choosing Luke as the writer of the Gospel that now bears his name or selecting John's name for the last of the New Testament Gospels? In mathematical terms, the answer would be pretty close to *zero*. In practical terms, the answer is, It ain't gonna happen, baby.

WHAT CAME WITH THE GOSPELS?

How, then, is it possible that the names of the authors are so consistent in the ancient manuscripts of the New Testament Gospels?

Consider this scenario: Let's suppose that, when each congregation received a copy of a Gospel, the congregation also received an *oral tradition* about the origins of that Gospel. And what if all the churches received and passed on the *same* oral traditions about the Gospels? As a result, when it became necessary to ascribe names and authors to the Gospels in their book-chests, every congregation connected the same authors' names with the same Gospels. Sure, the *exact form* of the titles differed, but the *names of the authors* remained identical.

Why?

Because each congregation had already received a consistent oral tradition about the source of each Gospel.

As it turns out, there *is* historical evidence that this is precisely what happened. For example, Papias of Hierapolis—a church leader in the geographic area known today as Turkey, born about the time the Gospels were being written and a friend of the four daughters of Philip[15]—preserved this tradition about the Gospels of Mark and Matthew:

> I won't hesitate to arrange alongside my interpretations whatever things I learned and remembered well from the elders, confirming the truth on their behalf. . . . The elder said this: Mark, who became Peter's interpreter, wrote accurately as much as he remembered—though not in ordered form—of the Lord's say-

ings and doings. For [Mark] neither heard the Lord nor followed after him, but later (as I said) he followed after Peter, who was giving his teachings in short anecdotes and thus did not bring forth an ordered arrangement of the Lord's sayings; so, Mark did not miss the point when he wrote in this way, as he remembered. For he had one purpose—to omit nothing of what he had heard and to present no false testimony in these things. . . . Matthew, in the Hebrew dialect, placed the sayings in orderly arrangement, and each one interpreted them as he was able.[16]

Only a few fragments of Papias's writings survive today. Consequently, it's possible that Papias recorded traditions about the other Gospels too, but those records have been lost. In any case, what *is* preserved from Papias shows that oral histories of the Gospels' origins ex-

---

LOOK IT UP

book-chest Place where early churches kept scrolls and codices of the Old Testament and of Christian writings that were read during worship celebrations.

---

isted in the final years of the first century, probably even earlier.[17]

Two decades after Papias's death in the mid-second century, a church leader named Irenaeus reported similar traditions that included not only the Gospels of Matthew and Mark but also those of Luke and John. Writing from a region of the Roman Empire now known as France, here's what Irenaeus had to say about the Gospels:

Matthew composed his Gospel among the Hebrews in their language, while Peter and Paul were preaching the Gospel in Rome

and building up the church there. After their deaths, Mark—
Peter's follower and interpreter—handed down to us Peter's
proclamation in written form. Luke, the companion of Paul,
wrote in a book the Gospel proclaimed by Paul. Finally, John—
the Lord's own follower, the one who leaned against his chest—
composed the Gospel while living in Ephesus, in Asia.[18]

And where had Irenaeus received his information? From his
teacher Polycarp, who received it from the eyewitnesses of Jesus.[19]
So, Papias and Irenaeus—two leaders in the early church, separated
by hundreds of miles and decades of time—reported nearly identical
traditions about two of the New Testament Gospels.[20] And there's

---

THINK IT OUT

Not surprisingly, Ehrman questions the accuracy of the traditions
that come from Papias. To understand *why* these traditions are still
valuable, check out the appendix at the end of this book, "How Valuable Is the Testimony of Papias?"

---

every reason to think that consistent traditions concerning the other
two Gospels were circulating at the same time.

What's more, a New Testament scholar named Claus-Jürgen
Thornton has demonstrated not only that the traditions found in Irenaeus exhibit every mark of authenticity but also that they are very
similar to the notes about authors that were kept in the catalogs of
ancient libraries.[21] This similarity suggests that some Christian congregations may even have maintained brief informational notes about
each codex in their book-chests.

KNOW MORE

Every known manuscript of the Gospel According to Matthew is written in Greek. Yet Papias and Irenaeus report that Matthew wrote his Gospel first and that he wrote in *Hebrew*. As a result, many scholars believe the apostle Matthew originally wrote Jesus' teachings in *Aramaic,* a language that's closely related to Hebrew. Later, someone— perhaps Matthew or someone associated with Matthew—merged these teachings with portions of Mark's Gospel to form the Gospel According to Matthew as we know it,[22] in the Greek language.[23] Such practices were not unheard-of in the first century: Flavius Josephus wrote two histories of the Jewish-Roman War, one in Aramaic and the other in Greek. As with Matthew's Gospel, the Aramaic version didn't circulate widely and, thus, has not survived.[24] The book of Tobit—found in Roman Catholic and Eastern Orthodox Bibles—was also thought for many years to have circulated only in Greek. Recently, fragments of separate Hebrew and Aramaic versions of this book have been discovered among the Dead Sea Scrolls.[25]

So, is Ehrman correct when he claims that second-century churches simply ascribed four anonymous Gospels to well-known Christians whose names would be perceived as authoritative? If that had been the pattern for naming the New Testament Gospels, there would have been many—perhaps dozens—of different authors' names found on the four Gospels. *Yet no such pattern can be found anywhere in the ancient manuscripts.* The authors connected with the New Testament Gospels consistently remain the same from one manuscript to another. Why? Because, when the churches received the written Gospels, they received more than mere documents. They also received *stories*—oral histories from the first century A.D.—about each Gospel's origins. These traditions stemmed from the first readers of the Gospels and remained consistent as the Gospels made their way to every corner of the Roman Empire. From my perspective, nothing less can reasonably explain the remarkable uniformity of authors' names in the Gospel manuscripts.

TRUTH ABOUT
EYEWITNESS TESTIMONY

Even though we might desperately want to know the
identities of the authors of the earliest Gospels, we sim-
ply don't have sufficient evidence. The books were writ-
ten anonymously and evidently not by eyewitnesses.

BART D. EHRMAN

How do you know that you were born? I mean, simply because
you're here right now doesn't *prove* that you were born. Perhaps there
are other ways to arrive on this planet. And you don't *remember* being
born, do you?

So, how do you know that you were born?

You have witnesses? Oh yes, your mother, and maybe a doctor,
your father, a few nurses. But have your parents *ever* lied? How about
medical personnel? Who's to say they aren't lying now, trying to hide
some dark secret about how you really arrived?

You have documents? Oh yes, the birth certificate. But documents
can be falsified, you know.

And pictures? Oh yes, the photo from the maternity ward, the one
that shows a red-splotched newborn with a hospital bracelet around
its wrist. But how do you know that's *you?* Who's to say that the infant

in the photograph is even real? Anyone with access to photo-editing software can create a false picture after all.

At this point, a few of you are thinking, Oh no! What if I *wasn't* born? What if by some biological fluke, I was spawned in a pond amid the tadpoles and dragonflies? Or maybe I was a blue-light special at K-Mart! If that's what's going through your mind, breathe deeply and don't despair. I am quite convinced that you *were* born— but I want to make a point about how we determine historical truth.

Here's my point: You cannot absolutely prove that *any* past event actually occurred. Records can be forged, people can make mistakes, and you can't replicate a past event in a laboratory—a past event has, by definition, *passed.* So, how do you decide whether something happened in the past?

Even though no single record or testimony can prove by itself that a past event happened, each witness increases the *probability* that certain events did occur. And the most valuable testimonies come from eyewitnesses—from people that were present when the past event happened.

As it turns out, proving your personal nativity doesn't particularly concern me; I'm perfectly willing to *assume* that you were born. But what if, for some reason, I *did* need to make certain that you were born? Together, a birth certificate, the doctor's report from the day of your alleged birth and sworn affidavits from both of your parents would incline me to believe your claims about your birthday—even though I know that forgeries *are* possible.

If I could speak personally with some of these supposed witnesses, I would feel even more confident about how you arrived on this planet, especially if they seemed to be generally trustworthy people. Granted, none of these witnesses would prove your birth beyond any possible doubt, but each one *would* increase my confidence that you were born. Taken together, they would most likely lift my confidence in your birth to the level of overwhelming probability.

So what's my point in all of this? *You can't prove that past events happened.* What you *can* do is look carefully at artifacts and testimonies from past events—especially reports from eyewitnesses—and determine which purported events are most probable. That's how historians decide whether to believe that Caesar Augustus once ruled the Roman Empire, that the American Civil War claimed more than 500,000 lives and that human birth was the probable pathway by which you arrived on this planet. In each of these cases, records that come from eyewitnesses provide the strongest evidences that these events *did* happen.

THE IMPORTANCE OF EYEWITNESSES

The first followers of Jesus also understood the importance of reliable eyewitnesses—especially when they began to claim that Jesus had returned from the dead. This claim *is,* after all, quite incredible. As a result, early Christians cherished eyewitness testimonies about the resurrection.

Two New Testament Gospels specifically claim that eyewitness reports formed the foundation for what they had to say about Jesus. "These things were handed down to us," the preface of the Gospel According to Luke declares, "by those who were eyewitnesses from the beginning" (Luke 1:2; see also Acts 1:22). And the writer of John's Gospel announced with utmost sincerity, "The one who saw this has testified—his testimony is true, and he knows he is telling the truth" (John 19:35; see also 21:24). Around A.D. 160, an unknown writer in Rome recorded an oral tradition that backed up these claims. According to this author, Luke based his Gospel on personal interviews, presumably with eyewitnesses, and the Fourth Gospel represented the eyewitness testimony of the apostle John.[1]

The other two Gospels don't specifically claim to come from eye-witnesses,[2] but early Christians believed that these writings repre-sented eyewitness testimony. Writing from Asia Minor in the early second century, Papias of Hierapolis affirmed that Mark's Gospel pre-served Peter's eyewitness testimony and that the apostle Matthew was responsible for the Gospel that bore his name. A few years later, Ire-naeus of Lyons—the leading pastor in an area known today as north-ern France—linked each New Testament Gospel to an eyewitness of the resurrected Lord.[3] Justin—a defender of Christian faith, writing from Rome in the mid-second century—referred to a quotation from Mark 3:16-17 as coming from the "recollections of Peter."[4] Around A.D. 200, Tertullian of Carthage put it this way:

> We present as our first position, that the Gospel testimony has apostles for its authors, to whom the Lord himself assigned the position of propagating the Gospel. There are also some that, though not *apostles,* are *apostolic*—they do not stand alone; they appear with and after the apostles. . . . So, John and Matthew, of the apostles, first instill faith into us while the apostolic writ-ers Luke and Mark renew it afterwards. . . . Never mind that there occurs some variation in the order of their narratives, as long as there is agreement in essential matters of faith.[5]

From the first century onward, a consistent strand of Christian tra-dition tied the truth of the New Testament Gospels to eyewitness tes-timony.[6]

NOT BY PEOPLE WHO WERE EYEWITNESSES?

Despite the consistent testimony of Christian writers throughout the first and second centuries, Ehrman flatly denies that the New Testament could have been written by eye witnesses:

> [The Gospels] were written thirty-five to sixty-five years after
> Jesus' death, . . . not by people who were eyewitnesses, but by
> people living later. . . . After the days of Jesus, people started
> telling stories about him in order to convert others to the faith.[7]

In the last chapter, you learned that, even though the first copies
of the New Testament Gospels *may* have been anonymous, these
Gospels circulated with consistent oral traditions about their authors.
Now, it's time to ask the next logical question: Were these oral tra-

---

KNOW MORE

The first known listing of Christian writings that should be considered authoritative is *the Muratorian Canon*—so called because it's
recorded on a fragment discovered by a man named Ludovico Muratori in around 1740. No one knows who recorded this list, though the
list seems to have been written near Rome around A.D. 160. The Muratorian Canon includes all the books that appear in the New Testament today except Hebrews, James, 1 and 2 Peter, and 2 and 3 John.
According to the Muratorian Fragment, Luke based his Gospel on personal interviews, presumably with eyewitnesses, and the Fourth
Gospel represented the eyewitness testimony of the apostle John.

---

ditions *true?* And, supposing they were true, how likely is it that what
stands behind the New Testament Gospels is eyewitness testimony?
Is it possible that the traditional ascriptions are true? Or is Ehrman
correct when he declares that the Gospels must be the result of tales
told later by people who never actually saw Jesus of Nazareth?

It's important to note at this point that the truth of the four New Testament Gospels *doesn't* depend on the accuracy of the traditional ascriptions of the books to Matthew, Mark, Luke and John. In other words, the Gospels might represent historical truth even if these four authors didn't write the books that bear their names. At the same time, if the traditional ascriptions *are* correct, the likelihood that the Gospels were based on eyewitness testimony becomes more probable.

WHO WAS STILL ALIVE?

So, what are the chances that eyewitness evidences formed the foundations of the four New Testament Gospels? Most scholars admit that all four New Testament Gospels were written sometime between A.D. 50 and 100. Based on the content and language in each Gospel, the majority of New Testament scholars would agree with the ranges that Ehrman assigns to the emergence of the Gospels: The Gospel According to Mark came into existence between 65 and 70, the Gospels According to Matthew and Luke emerged a decade or so later, and John's Gospel was completed sometime before A.D. 95.[8]

When I look at these dates, here's what I find interesting: *Some of the people who walked and talked with Jesus must have been alive when the first Gospels were written.* Writing a letter to the Corinthians two decades or so after Jesus trudged up the Hill of the Skull, the apostle Paul could say, "[The Lord] was seen by more than five hundred brothers at once, most of whom are still living, though some have fallen asleep" (1 Corinthians 15:6). If Mark's Gospel first began to circulate around A.D. 70, it's virtually certain that some of these people who had seen the risen Jesus would still have been alive. A few years later, when clusters of Christians throughout the Roman Empire began to read the three later New Testament Gospels, it's not at all unlikely that at least a few acquaintances of Jesus were still breathing.

Thus it's a bit of a stretch to state, without qualification, that the four Gospels were penned "not by people who were eyewitnesses, but by people living later,"[9] as Ehrman does. If the Gospels began to circulate three or four decades after Jesus walked this earth, it is at least *possible* that the sources of these books were eyewitnesses of Jesus. The emergence of Mark's Gospel only thirty years or so after Jesus' death makes it difficult to deny that eyewitness testimony, at the very least, was *available* to the authors of the Gospels.[10]

HOW DUMB WERE THE DISCIPLES?

So what proof does Ehrman offer for his unreserved claim that the New Testament Gospels were *not* based on eyewitness testimony?[11] Simply this:

Jesus' own followers . . . were mainly lower-class peasants— fishermen and artisans, for example—and . . . they spoke Aramaic rather than Greek. If they *did* have any kind of facility in Greek, it would have been simply for rough communication at best (kind of like when I bungle my way through Germany, to the general consternation of native speakers). Even more strikingly, the two leaders among Jesus' followers, Peter and John, are explicitly said in the New Testament to be "illiterate." [Acts 4:13] . . . In the end, it seems unlikely that the uneducated, lower-class, illiterate disciples of Jesus played the decisive role in the literary compositions that have come down through history under their names.[12]

At first glance, Ehrman's reconstruction is convincing. After all, he *is* correct that some members of the Judean ruling council pointed out that Peter and John were *agrammatoi* or "unschooled" (Acts 4:13). How, then, could such testimony—stories that may have circulated first in coarse Aramaic—have turned into the Greek documents found in the New Testament Gospels today?

The first difficulty with Ehrman's interpretation is that the word *agrammatos* does *not* necessarily imply that Peter and John were illiterate. In the context of the Jewish council, *agrammatos* likely meant "untrained in the Jewish law."[13] If this is the case, the council members were pointing out that, despite their boldness in interpreting the Hebrew Scriptures, Peter and John had not been schooled as rabbis.[14]

So, were the traditional authors of the four New Testament Gospels "illiterate," as Ehrman claims? Were they really incapable of creating works of literature? Or, was there something more going on in the first century than Ehrman has revealed to his readers? Let's take a look at each of the traditional authors and see where Ehrman is correct—and where a few additional facts may help us to look at Ehrman's reconstructions in a new light.

WHAT TAX COLLECTORS COULD DO

In the book that bears his name, Matthew is presented as a "publican" or "tax collector."[15] It's doubtful that any early Christian would have fabricated this bit of vocational trivia. After all, the very idea that Jesus asked a tax collector to follow him must have been a bit embarrassing. When the Gospels were written, Roman governors expected tax collectors to stockpile personal wealth by cheating people—and most tax collectors apparently complied with this expectation. Not surprisingly, tax collectors rarely made it to the top of anyone's list of most-loved citizens.

In Roman rhetoric, to refer to someone as a tax collector was to call that person's honor into question.[16] In the writings of Josephus, the Jewish historian told how a Judean tax collector bribed the corrupt governor Florus not long before Florus incited the Jewish rebellion against Rome.[17] And, according to the Gospels, folk in Judea and Galilee grouped tax collectors with drunkards, gluttons, pagans and adulterers (Matthew 11:19; 18:17; Luke 18:11). Simply put, answering the classified ad that read "Become a Roman tax collector! Make millions fleecing your friends!" was *not* the most promising pathway to personal popularity in the ancient world.

But there was one skill that tax collectors *did* possess.

They could read and write.

Tax collectors were, in fact, known to carry *pinakes,* hinged wooden tablets with a thick wax coating on each panel.[18] Tax collectors used styluses of metal or bone to etch notes in the wax—notes that, in some cases, were later translated and rewritten on papyrus.[19] Papyri from Egypt prove that tax collectors also wrote receipts and registers for citizens in their villages.[20]

Despite Ehrman's disdainful description of the first disciples as "uneducated, lower-class, illiterate,"[21] a tax collector such as Matthew could *not* have fit such a description. The daily tasks of a Galilean tax collector required him to collect, copy and record information, probably in multiple languages.

KNOW MORE

"The Romans ... deliberately choose ruthless and savage people as tax collectors; then, they provide them with ways to satisfy their greed.... They leave no cruelty untried, refusing to recognize any form of fairness or gentleness.... They spread confusion and chaos everywhere. They exact money not only from people's property but also from their bodies by means of injuries, assaults, and unheard-of tortures."[22]

Philo of Alexandria

WHAT COULD PHYSICIANS WRITE?

What about another character whose name is ascribed to a Gospel, the companion of Paul named Luke? Compared to other people in the New Testament, Luke is a quite obscure character. He's mentioned only three times in letters attributed to Paul (Colossians 4:14; Philemon 1:24; 2 Timothy 4:11). Considering how many of Paul's partners enjoy far greater prominence in the New Testament—Timothy, for example, or Barnabas or Silas—it's difficult to explain why anyone would ascribe the third Gospel to Luke . . . unless, of course, Luke actually *was* responsible for the book that bears his name. At the very least, it seems that Luke's authorship is a possibility worth examining.

According to an ancient letter to the church in Colossae, Luke was Paul's "beloved physician" (Colossians 4:14). Physicians in the ancient world didn't enjoy quite the affluence or esteem that they do today. Most physicians received their training by becoming apprentices of a more experienced physician—frequently the aspiring physician's father—until they learned the art of medicine.[23] Outside the training of medics in the Roman military, no fixed curriculum existed for the training of ancient medical practitioners.[24] Consequently, it's difficult to determine the precise extent of literacy among physicians.

KNOW MORE

"Since many have put their hands to arrange a guided presentation about the deeds that have been fully carried out among us, just as eyewitnesses and subordinates of this message have handed them on to us, it seemed good to me also . . . to write them."

Luke 1:1-3

Still, a physician would seem to have possessed, at the very least, the capacity to read the summaries of medical knowledge that flourished in the first century. What's more, papyri from Egypt prove that ancient physicians and their scribes frequently wrote reports for law-enforcement officials regarding suspicious injuries and possible causes of death, as well as statements for slave masters certifying the health of slaves.[25] So—if indeed Luke was a physician, as the letter to the Colossians suggests—it's unlikely that he was "illiterate" or "uneducated." And many physicians were capable of pulling together various eyewitness accounts into a coherent report, just as the preface of Luke's Gospel implies that the author has done.

WHAT ABOUT MARK AND JOHN?

That leaves Mark and John. When it comes to these two witnesses, Ehrman may be correct: Though it is by no means certain, either or both of these men may have been illiterate. Yet even this doesn't preclude the possibility that eyewitness sources stand behind the New Testament Gospels.

In the first century A.D., professional scribes were readily available to render messages from other languages, including Aramaic, into polished Greek. Complex legal titles, eloquent epistles to family members and simple commercial receipts all required secretarial skills—and provided livelihoods for a multitude of scribes not only in urban areas such as Ephesus and Rome but also in Galilee and Judea. And prosperous patrons weren't the only people that used professional scribes; persons from poorer classes employed scribes too.[26] Even though Paul was completely capable of writing in Greek (Galatians 6:11; Philemon 1:19-21), scribes penned Paul's letters for him (Romans 16:22; see also 1 Peter 5:12).[27]

It's entirely possible that Mark and John employed professional scribes to render their oral accounts of Jesus' life into the Greek documents that centuries of copyists have passed down to us. If so, they would still have been the *sources* of these Gospels, even if they didn't pen the actual words.[28]

I do find it intriguing that the simplest Greek in the New Testament is found in the Gospel According to John and the Gospel According to Mark, the two Gospels whose traditional authors *might* have been less than literate. In fact—even after translating hundreds of Greek epigraphs, papyri and writings from prominent second- and third-century Christians—I still haven't found a document written as simply as the Gospel According to John.

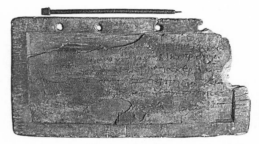

An ancient wax tablet (*pinax*) with bronze stylus. (Photograph MS608 courtesy of The Schøyen Collection, Oslo and London.)

When I teach Greek to college and seminary students, I expect students to be able to translate all of John's Gospel and most of Mark's Gospel with minimal assistance after only nine months in the texts—and, with very few exceptions, they can! (And, by the way, if you're one of the handful that *couldn't,* I do hope that your grade-point average eventually recovered.) Perhaps the simplicity of these two Gospels stems from their origins—spoken words flowing from the tongues of two ordinary men whose stories a scribe shaped, arranged and preserved in papyrus and ink.

WHY I STILL CELEBRATE MY BIRTHDAY

So, what about Ehrman's claim that the New Testament Gospels do not represent eyewitness testimony about Jesus of Nazareth?

Based on the dates when the Gospels were written, it's nearly impossible to deny that eyewitness testimony *may have been* available to the authors of these documents. What's more, Ehrman's claim that the traditional authors of the Gospels couldn't have been the sources of these books because these four men were "uneducated, lower-class, [and] illiterate" is simply untrue. Matthew the tax collector and Luke the physician almost certainly would have possessed the capacity to author such documents, and, even if Mark and John *were* illiterate, professional scribes were readily available to them.

In the end, I find no compelling reason to reject the ancient oral traditions that connected the New Testament Gospels to Matthew, Mark, Luke and John. Given the evidence that's available to us, no one can be certain who wrote these books—in this, Ehrman is correct. And, still, the best evidence that we possess suggests that the sources for the four Gospels were a tax collector named Matthew, Simon Peter's translator Mark, the physician Luke and a fisherman named John.

Do I know this for certain?

Well, no.

But, then again, I don't *know* that I was born either. Yet the best evidence that I possess compels me to believe I *was* born. So, each year on the sixteenth of January, I celebrate that belief with a completely clear conscience. Historical evidence also compels me to think that Matthew, Mark, Luke and John were the sources of the books that bear their names. So, whenever I open my New Testament to the Gospels, I read these documents with a clear conscience as the words of these four witnesses.

If indeed Matthew, Mark, Luke and John *were* the sources of the books that bear their names—and I think that they most likely were—each New Testament Gospel represents eyewitness testimony about Jesus. What's recorded in the Gospel According to Mark is the testimony of Simon Peter, recalled and preserved by John Mark. Luke's Gospel integrates written and oral sources gathered by Paul's personal physician. The materials that are unique to the Gospel According to Matthew came from Matthew, a tax collector who deserted a profitable profession to follow Jesus. And the stories in the Gospel According to John? It seems that they originated in John Bar-Zebedee—one of Jesus' first followers—or perhaps one of John's students, recording his teacher's testimony.

8

TRUTH ABOUT HOW
THE BOOKS WERE CHOSEN

*Many Christians today may think that the canon of the
New Testament simply appeared on the scene one day,
soon after the death of Jesus, but nothing could be far-
ther from the truth.*

BART D. EHRMAN

To understand why eyewitness testimony mattered so much to early
Christians, let's suppose for a moment that you're a Christian in the
mid-second century—say, somewhere around A.D. 160.

The last eyewitnesses of Jesus' resurrection died a generation ago.
For nearly a century, Christians in your town have gathered each
week in the courtyard of a wealthier believer's villa. In a wooden cabinet in the villa, your congregation's host keeps a Greek translation of
the Jewish Scriptures, as well as two dozen or so codices that your
congregation cherishes.

These codices are your copies of the writings of the first followers
of Jesus—many of whom died for their faith when emperors such as
Nero and Domitian demanded the persecution of Christians in the
provinces of Asia and Italia. There are not only books about Jesus and
his first followers but also letters from apostles such as Peter, Paul

and John. Each week, when your congregation gathers, one of your leaders reads selections from these writings.

But there *have* been questions about a few texts.

The questions began when a visiting teacher brought some new codices—a Gospel that claims to come from Peter, a book about the afterlife that's also ascribed to Peter, a vision mediated through a divine being in a shepherd's outfit and a handy manual that claims to contain *The Teaching of the Twelve Apostles.* Plus, there are several letters that scribes in nearby congregations were kind enough to copy for your church. There's a second letter from Simon Peter, a note from a leader in the Roman church named Clement and an epistle that claims to come from Barnabas. Not everyone is certain what to do with these writings. Should the church's leaders read them alongside the Gospels, the letters of Paul and the Jewish Scriptures? If so, is everyone in the church required to follow everything that they suggest?

Then, there are the rumors from the city of Rome. A leatherworker from your congregation just returned from the city of the Senate and the Caesars. After spending his days selling goat-hides in the marketplace, he listened to several lectures from an energetic preacher named Marcion. According to Marcion, the only books that belonged in Christians' book-chests were the epistles of Paul and the Gospel According to Luke. And, then, Marcion even argued that some portions of Luke's Gospel should be cut out!

Now, the leather-worker is convinced that at least a few codices in your church's book-chest may not be trustworthy. At the very least, he says, not all of them are equal. Surely the words of Jesus himself and his first followers are more important than later letters from other pastors! And, now, a handful of people wonder if Marcion might be correct: Perhaps the only books that belong in your book-chest *are* Paul's letters and the Gospel According to Luke.

LOOK IT UP

Marcion of Sinope (died around A.D. 160) Believing that the Jewish people had misunderstood God's revelation and that the physical world was intrinsically evil, Marcion created a list of authoritative books to fit his theology. This list included heavily edited versions of Luke's Gospel and of Paul's epistles. He began teaching in Rome around A.D. 140; the church in Rome excluded him from fellowship in 144.

HOW DID THE CHURCHES AGREE?

Do you sense the dilemma that faced second-century churches as more and more Christian writings began to circulate? As new writings surfaced, Christians had to decide which documents represented the truth about Jesus and what sort of clout these writings should command in their day-by-day lives. So how did early believers make this decision?

Here's how the churches decided which writings were authoritative, according to Ehrman's explanation in *Misquoting Jesus:*

We are able to pinpoint the first time that any Christian of record listed the twenty-seven books of our New Testament as *the* books of the New Testament—neither more nor fewer. Surprising as it may seem, this Christian was writing in the second half of the fourth century, nearly three hundred years after the books of the New Testament had themselves been written. The author was the powerful bishop of Alexandria named Athanasius. In the year 367 C.E., Athanasius wrote his annual pastoral letter to the Egyptian churches under his jurisdiction, and in it he included advice concerning which books should be read as Scripture in the churches. He lists our twenty-seven books, excluding all others. This is the first surviving instance of anyone affirming our set of books as the New Testament. And even Athanasius did not settle the matter. Debates continued for decades, even centuries.[1]

Every fact that Ehrman provides in this summary is true—but he also leaves out a few key truths. As a result, Ehrman's summary could leave readers with a couple of impressions that aren't quite correct—impressions such as, (1) until the late fourth century, there was no consensus about which Christian writings were authoritative and true, and (2) even then the church's standard was simply the word of a powerful bishop.

So what's the complete truth? When *did* Christians agree on which writings were authoritative in their congregations? And what were the standards for these decisions?

In the first place, the primary standard for deciding which books were authoritative emerged long before the fourth century—and the standard *wasn't* the word of a powerful bishop. Hints of this standard can, in fact, be found in first-century Christian writings. Although no one put this standard into writing, the basic idea was something like this: *Testimony that could be connected to eyewitnesses of the risen Lord was uniquely authoritative among early Christians.*[2]

WHY THE EYEWITNESSES MATTERED

Even while the New Testament books were being written, the words of people who saw and followed the risen Lord—especially the words and writings of the apostles—carried special authority in the churches (see Acts 1:21-26; 15:6–16:5; 1 Corinthians 4–5; 9:1-12;

Galatians 1:1-12; 1 Thessalonians 5:26-27). After the apostles' deaths, Christians continued to cherish the testimony of eyewitnesses and their associates. Around A.D. 110, Papias of Hierapolis put it this way:

> I did not . . . take pleasure in those who spoke much, but in those who taught truth—not in those who related strange commandments, but in those who recited the commandments given by the Lord. . . . So, if anyone who had served the elders came, I asked about their sayings in detail—what Andrew or Peter said, or what was said by Philip or Thomas or James or John or Matthew or any other of the Lord's followers.[3]

About the same time, a church leader named Polycarp cited the words of the apostle Paul as "Scripture."[4]

A generation later, when someone in the Roman church considered which Christian writings should be authoritative, this emphasis on the apostolic eyewitnesses persisted. After listing the books that he viewed as authoritative, here's what one Christian wrote regarding a popular book known as *The Shepherd* that was circulating in the churches:

> Hermas composed *The Shepherd* quite recently—in our times, in the city of Rome, while his brother Pius the overseer served as overseer of the city of Rome. So, while it should indeed be read, it cannot be read publicly for the people of the church—it is counted neither among the Prophets (for their number has been completed) nor among the Apostles (for it is after their time).[5]

Notice carefully this second-century writer's reasons for not allowing *The Shepherd* of Hermas to serve as an authoritative guideline in the churches: This writing could not be added to the Old Testament prophets because the time of the Hebrew prophets had passed ("their number has been completed"), and—with the deaths of the apostles—the time of the apostolic eyewitnesses had also ended ("it is after their time"). This teacher didn't forbid believers to read *The Shepherd*; he simply pointed out that the book should not serve as an authoritative text for Christian congregations ("it cannot be read publicly for the people of the church").

Later church leaders such as Tertullian of Carthage and Serapion of Antioch echoed these sorts of standards, with Serapion clearly stating, "We, brothers and sisters, receive Peter and the rest of the apostles as we would receive Christ himself. But those writings that are falsely ascribed with their names, we carefully reject, knowing that no such writings have ever been handed down to us."[6] Again, Christians rooted their standard for determining which writings were authoritative in the testimony of apostolic eyewitnesses.

From the first century onward, Christians viewed testimony that could be connected to eyewitnesses of the risen Lord as uniquely authoritative. The logic of this standard was simple: The people most likely to know the truth about Jesus were either eyewitnesses who

---

KNOW MORE

The Shepherd of Hermas is a lengthy and somewhat odd allegory related through a series of visions. The book was most likely written in the mid-second century A.D. The author's specific beliefs about Jesus and the Holy Spirit are vague, and some passages could be construed to mean that Jesus somehow *became* the Son of God instead of *always having been* the divine Son. Still, *The Shepherd* remained a popular devotional book for many second- and third-century Christians.

---

had encountered Jesus personally or close associates of these witnesses. So, although Christians wrangled for several centuries about *which* writings were authoritative, it was something much greater than political machinations that drove their decisions. Their goal was to determine which books could be connected to eyewitnesses of the risen Lord.

With this in mind, let's look at a couple of real-life examples of how some writings ended up excluded from the churches' collections of authoritative books!

GOSPEL OF PETER: THE GOSPEL OF THE TALKING CROSS

In A.D. 199, a pastor named Serapion became overseer of the leading church in Syria, the church in Antioch. As pastor in Antioch, Serapion was responsible not only for his own church but also for several smaller congregations in the area. One of these congregations gathered in the village of Rhossus. Within a few months, Serapion heard rumors that the church in Rhossus was on the verge of a rift, so Serapion found himself trudging the stony coastal road that took him north of Antioch, toward Rhossus.

When he arrived in Rhossus, he discovered that some church members had problems with a Gospel that was "inscribed with Peter's name."[7] When he heard this, Serapion replied, "If that's all that threatens to produce hard feelings among you, let it be read." After all, if this retelling of Jesus' ministry came from Simon Peter, surely it represented eyewitness testimony! Given the consistent tradition in the early church that the Gospel According to Mark represented Peter's account of Jesus' life, it's even possible that Serapion assumed the good folk at Rhossus were describing Mark's Gospel.

In any case, the answer wasn't nearly as clear-cut as Serapion thought. Some time later, someone brought the pastor a copy of *Gos-*

pel of Peter. When Serapion read the codex for himself, he recognized he'd made a serious mistake. Sure, most of *Gospel of Peter* reflected the same stories as the other writings in the church's book-chest. Little—if anything—in the available manuscripts of *Gospel of Peter* directly contradicts the New Testament Gospels.

And yet, Serapion saw that this book was clearly *not* the product of Simon Peter's preaching.[8] There were hints of the beginnings of a false belief that emerged near the end of the first century, a couple of decades after Peter's death. This heresy—known as *Docetism,* from the Greek word *dokein* ("to seem")—claimed that Jesus wasn't truly human; instead, according to these teachers, Jesus only *seemed* human. For example, when *Gospel of Peter* describes the crucifixion, it suggests that Jesus "was quiet, as if he felt no pain."[9] The intent of this phrase is probably to point out the Messiah's calmness on the cross, echoing a line from Isaiah 53:7: "Like a sheep that before its shearers is silent, so he did not open his mouth." And it doesn't say that Jesus felt no pain—it states that he reacted "*as if* he felt no pain." Still, the Docetists could twist this passage to mean that Jesus felt no physical pain, and, therefore, he must not have possessed a physical body.

There are a handful of other oddities in *Gospel of Peter.* When Jesus died, *Gospel of Peter* says simply that "he was taken up." But, since *Gospel of Peter* describes a physical resurrection a few verses later, this was most likely another way of saying, with the New Testament Gospels, "he let go of [or, *gave up*] his spirit" (Matthew 27:50; cf. John 19:30).

The oddest twist in *Gospel of Peter* is when Jesus erupts from the tomb. In the soldiers' eyes, Jesus seems as tall as the sky, and, behind Jesus, they glimpse what looks like a massive cross. A voice thunders from heaven, "Have you proclaimed to those that are asleep?" To this, the cross replies, "Yes."

After reading *Gospel of Peter,* Serapion dashed off a letter to the church in Rhossus, reversing his previous decision and declaring, "I am hurrying to see you; expect to see me shortly. . . . Most things [in this Gospel] are from the Savior's right word, but some things are false—and these we will point out for you."

So, why did Serapion of Antioch reject *Gospel of Peter?* Ehrman makes much of Serapion's censure, claiming that the overseer of Antioch rejected the book simply because it failed to fit his preconceived notions about the identity of Jesus. According to Ehrman,

> Serapion concluded that because the book was potentially heretical, it must not have been written by Peter—operating on the dubious assumption that if a text disagreed with the truth as he and his fellow proto-orthodox Christians saw it, then it could not possibly be apostolic.[10]

Despite Ehrman's denunciation of his logic as "dubious," Serapion's reasoning is actually quite sound. Serapion had received, according to his letter to the church in Rhossus, the testimony of apostolic eyewitnesses "in the writings handed down to us."[11] These writings most likely included the letters of Paul and one or more of the New Testament Gospels, including the eyewitness recollections of Peter in the Gospel of Mark—documents that strong oral traditions had long linked to apostolic witnesses.

Faced with a writing that claimed to come from Simon Peter, Serapion compared its teachings with these "writings handed down to us" and found potential inconsistencies between *Gospel of Peter* and writings such as Mark's Gospel and 1 Peter, books that oral tradition had long linked to Simon Peter. As a result, Serapion reached the logical conclusion that Simon Peter—an apostolic eyewitness of Jesus, according to Paul's letters and the earliest Gospels—couldn't have been the source of the so-called *Gospel of Peter.* Serapion's goal was the same as fellow believers scattered throughout the world: He wanted to preserve eyewitness testimony about Jesus. When he examined *Gospel of Peter,* his conclusion was that this document didn't represent eyewitness testimony at all.

As it turns out, Serapion was correct: The language and thought-patterns in *Gospel of Peter* have convinced most contemporary scholars that the book was written in the first half of the second century—a generation after Peter's death, at a time when Docetist teachings were spreading.[12]

THINK IT OUT

Here's how *Gospel of Peter* describes the resurrection of Jesus: "The soldiers . . . saw the sky open, and two men descending from there. The men, shining brightly, came near the tomb. The stone pushed before the entrance rolled away of its own accord, moving aside. The tomb being opened, the young men entered. When the soldiers saw these things, they awakened the centurion and the elders—for they too were guarding the tomb. While they were explaining what they had seen, they saw three men come out of the tomb, two of them supporting the other and a cross coming behind them. The heads of the two reached toward the heavens, but the head of the one being led reached beyond the heavens. They heard a voice from the heavens, saying, 'Have you proclaimed to those that are asleep?' And a voice came from the cross, 'Yes.'"[13] What are the *differences* and the *similarities* between this story and the resurrection accounts in Matthew, Mark, Luke and John? Does anything about this account actually *contradict* Matthew, Mark, Luke or John?

Despite Serapion's rejection of the book, *Gospel of Peter* remained popular reading among Christians for several centuries. In fact, more ancient fragments remain from *Gospel of Peter* than from the Gospel According to Mark. A piece of broken pottery from the sixth or seventh century A.D. declares on one side "Peter, saint, evangelist" and on the other side "Let us receive his Gospel," though it's not completely clear whether "his Gospel" refers to the document known as *Gospel of Peter* or to Peter's preaching about Jesus. A copy of *Gospel of Peter* has even been found buried with a seventh-century Egyptian monk.[14] Still, only the scantest evidence exists to suggest that, except for those few months in the church at Rhossus, *Gospel of Peter* was ever considered an authoritative account of Jesus' life.[15]

ACTS OF PAUL: WHY YOUR CHURCH DOESN'T BAPTIZE LIONS

Around A.D. 200, an argument about baptism erupted in a congregation in North Africa. Some church members appealed to a writing known as *Acts of Paul*—a document that some Christians seem to have accepted as authoritative. And, I must admit, there are portions of *Acts of Paul* that would have provoked some interesting discussions during the Bible studies at your church.

According to this document, being a Christian includes not only faith in Jesus Christ but also complete abstinence from sexual relations, even within marriage. Plus, about halfway through *Acts of Paul*, the apostle Paul baptizes a lion that's eighteen feet tall. So, if *Acts of Paul* had ended up in the New Testament, you might get to dunk wild felines in your church's baptistery, but you'd also have to stop having sex. (Yeah, I know—so much for following Jesus.) Mostly, the book is a series of bizarre tales about how the apostle Paul and a woman named Thecla triumph over every possible plot to stop their proclamation of the Gospel.

It's an elder named Tertullian of Carthage who relates some of the reasons why *Acts of Paul* never became an authoritative text for Christians.[16] When Tertullian heard that some church members were appealing to

Acts of Paul as an authoritative portrayal of Paul's ministry, he seems to have done some research into the book's origins. In the process, he dug up several facts that cast doubt on the book's dependability.

Tertullian discovered that the author of *Acts of Paul* was neither an apostle nor acquainted with any apostles. The author had served as an elder in a church in Asia forty years or more after Paul's martyrdom.[17] When questioned, the elder contended that he concocted the stories "out of love for Paul."[18] Once churches in the area learned that these stories were pious fantasies, they forced the elder to step down from his position. This rightly led Tertullian to reject *Acts of Paul* as "a writing that circulates falsely under Paul's name."[19]

This third-century A.D. fragment is the oldest known portion of the *Acts of Paul and Thecla*. (Photograph of MS2634/1 courtesy of The Schøyen Collection, Oslo and London.)

What interests me most about the events surrounding *Acts of Paul* isn't why anyone would want to believe that Paul actually baptized a lion in the first place—though that question *does* cross my mind. What really intrigues me is how much early Christians wanted to make certain that their authoritative writings represented historical truth. It *mattered* to these men and women that historical facts actually formed the foundations of their sacred books. If second-century

Christians weren't concerned with preserving eyewitness truth, why did the author of the *Acts of Paul*—who most likely wanted nothing more than to honor Paul's memory with a few super-fantastic tales—end up shamed and stripped of his ordination?

Even among the earliest Christians, testimony that could be connected to eyewitnesses of the risen Lord was uniquely authoritative. That's why the supposed "lost Scriptures" were lost—or, more precisely, why they were not preserved as carefully as the writings that appear in your New Testament today.

Not only *Gospel of Peter* but also other post-apostolic accounts of the life and teachings of Jesus—*Gospel of Judas, Gospel of Mary, Gospel of Philip, Gospel of the Egyptians, Gospel of the Savior, Gospel of Truth* and several others—emerged in the second and third centuries, long after the last apostles died. It's true that some portions of *Gospel of Peter* as well as *Gospel of Thomas*—another second-century Gospel that's falsely ascribed to an apostle—probably stem from eyewitness testi-

---

LOOK IT UP

Gnostics (From Greek, *ginōskō,* "I have knowledge") Sect that emerged within and separated from the Christian movement in the first and second centuries A.D. Gnostics claimed to possess secret knowledge about God that was unavailable to others. Gnostics viewed the physical world and its Creator—usually identified with the God of the Old Testament—as evil. As a result, most Gnostics rejected all physical pleasures. For Gnostics, Jesus Christ was not God in human flesh. He was a divine spirit in what appeared to be a human body; his mission was to free people from the constraints of the physical world.

mony about Jesus.[20] But these few first-century traditions have been heavily mingled with second- and third-century additions.

In most cases, early Christians knew that these documents came too late to represent eyewitness testimony about Jesus. That's why they rejected these texts as authoritative accounts of Jesus' life. The primary preservers of these later texts became sects—such as the Gnostics—that concerned themselves more with mystical interpreta-

---

LOOK IT UP

Nag Hammadi documents Collection of more than forty Gnostic documents, unearthed in the mid-1940s near Nag Hammadi, a village in Upper Egypt. Significant texts found at Nag Hammadi include *Coptic Apocalypse of Paul, Coptic Apocalypse of Peter, Apocryphon of John, Dialogue of the Savior, Coptic Gospel of the Egyptians, Gospel of Philip, Gospel of Thomas* and *Gospel of Truth*.

---

tions of Jesus' teachings than with the historical events of Jesus' life. The texts of one such sect were discovered in the 1940s near the Egyptian village of Nag Hammadi.

How the Canon Came to Be

I don't want to leave you with the false impression that Christians quickly and easily settled every debate about their sacred writings. Prior to the fifth century, when different congregations listed the writings that they treated as authoritative testimony about Jesus, the results were rarely identical. To see how these lists could vary from one place to another, look carefully at these three lists from three different times and places in table 1.

Table 1.

The Fragment of Muratori (mid-second century A.D., Rome)	Codex Claromontanus (late third century A.D., Egypt or North Africa)	Eusebius of Caesarea's Church History (early fourth century A.D., Palestine and Asia Minor)
Accepted	**Accepted**	**Accepted**
Matthew	Matthew	Matthew
Mark	Mark	Mark
Luke	Luke	Luke
John	John	John
Acts	Acts	Acts
Romans	Romans	Romans
1 and 2 Corinthians	1 and 2 Corinthians	1 and 2 Corinthians
Galatians	Galatians	Galatians
Ephesians	Ephesians	Ephesians
Philippians	Philippians	Philippians
Colossians	Colossians	Colossians
1 and 2 Thessalonians	1 and 2 Thessalonians	1 and 2 Thessalonians
1 and 2 Timothy	1 and 2 Timothy	1 and 2 Timothy
Titus	Titus	Titus
Philemon	Philemon	Philemon
1 John	Hebrews*	Hebrews
2-3 John (counted as one)	James	1 Peter
Jude	1 and 2 Peter	1 John
Revelation	1, 2, and 3 John	Revelation*
Wisdom of Solomon	Jude	
	Revelation	
Disputed	**Disputed**	**Disputed**
Apocalypse of Peter	*Apocalypse of Peter*	James
	Epistle of Barnabas	Jude
	The Shepherd of Hermas	2 Peter
	Acts of Paul	2 and 3 John
Rejected		**Rejected**
Laodiceans		*Apocalypse of Peter*
Alexandrians		*Acts of Paul*
The Shepherd of Hermas		*The Shepherd* of Hermas
		Epistle of Barnabas
		Teaching of Twelve Apostles
		Gospel of Peter
		Gospel of Thomas
		Gospel of Matthias
		Gospel of the Hebrews
		Acts of Andrew
		Acts of John

*indicates that this canon listing *may* have placed this writing in the list of disputed books

When looking at the lists in table 1, it's easy to focus on the few books that *might* or *might not* have made it into the New Testament. Before you become too concerned with what might be different if Christians had concluded that your favorite book of the New Testament didn't qualify, though, notice the overwhelming degree of *agreement* among these lists. At least as early as the second century A.D., there were twenty or so books that were *never* questioned—and these are the writings that reflect the most essential truths about Jesus. From the very beginning, Christians embraced four Gospels, the Acts of the Apostles, the letters of Paul and at least one letter from John. Even if this score of books had been the *only* documents that represented eyewitness testimony about Jesus, every vital truth of Christian faith would remain completely intact.

Arguments about a few writings—including the letters of Peter, John's second and third letters, and the letters of James and Jude—persisted beyond the second century. Still, by the closing years of the fourth century, Christians were arriving at widespread agreement concerning twenty-seven books—writings that they believed were based on eyewitness testimony about Jesus. The letter of Athanasius in A.D. 367—the epistle that, according to Ehrman, first urged "that our current twenty-seven books . . . be accepted as Scripture"—reflected this consensus.

For the most part, Ehrman is correct in his description of how the canon of Scripture came together. Many years *did* pass before Christians agreed concerning which books should compose their sacred Scriptures. And, yet, a definite standard directed this process—a conviction that these writings must be rooted in reliable, eyewitness testimony about Jesus Christ.

What's more, despite continuing disagreements about a few writings, strong agreement on twenty or so books existed at least as early as the second century. God never promised that the process of determining which books represented eyewitness testimony would be without error. Yet there's every reason to believe that the testimony I find in my New Testament accurately reflects the experiences of men and women who personally followed Jesus and who passed on their experiences to generations yet to come.

LOOK IT UP

canon (From the Greek noun *kanōn,* "measuring stick") Religious texts that are authoritative for members of that religion. Around twenty of the books in the New Testament were accepted as authoritative from the beginning. This list of unquestioned books included the four Gospels, the Acts of the Apostles, the thirteen letters of Paul and the first letter ascribed to John. Interestingly, even if the New Testament included only these books, every essential doctrine of the Christian faith would remain intact.

CONCLUDING REFLECTIONS
"It Fits the Lock"

In answer to the historical query of why [Christian faith] was accepted and is accepted, I answer for millions of others in my reply; because it fits the lock, because it is like life. It is one among many stories; only it happens to be a true story. . . . We accept it; and the ground is solid under our feet and the road is open before us. . . . It opens to us not only incredible heavens but what seems to some an equally incredible earth, and makes it credible. This is the sort of truth that is hard to explain because it is a fact; but it is a fact to which we can call witnesses. We are Christians . . . not because we worship a key, but because we have passed a door; and felt the wind that is the trumpet of liberty blow over the land of the living.

GILBERT KEITH CHESTERTON,
THE EVERLASTING MAN

After years of wrestling with the Gospels, I find myself continually returning to the same conclusion: As absurd as it may seem that God embraced human flesh to suffer death and to rise again, this story—in the words of G. K. Chesterton—"fits the lock." It simply *works*.

And it works not only at the level of satisfying the human heart but also in the context of history.

This is not to say that no difficulties or incongruities remain. There are portions of the Gospels that I still struggle to reconcile. Perhaps I always will. And yet, there remains a consistency among these documents that continues to thwart my attempts to explain away the story that they share.

Occasionally, it seems as if Ehrman glimpses this consistency too. In his recent book *Peter, Paul, and Mary Magdalene,* Ehrman admits,

> I am struck by a certain consistency among otherwise independent witnesses in placing Mary Magdalene both at the cross and at the tomb on the third day. If this is not a historical datum but something that a Christian storyteller made up and then passed along to others, how is it that this specific bit of information has found its way into accounts that otherwise did not make use of one another? Mary's presence at the cross is found in Mark (and in Luke and Matthew, which used Mark) and also in John, which is independent of Mark. More significant still, all of our early Gospels—not just John and Mark (with Matthew and Luke as well) but also the Gospel of Peter, which appears to be independent of all of them—indicate that it was Mary Magdalene who discovered Jesus' empty tomb. How did all of these independent accounts happen to name exactly the same person in this role? It seems hard to believe that this just happened by way of a fluke of storytelling. It seems much more likely that, at least with the traditions involving the empty tomb, we are dealing with something actually rooted in history.[1]

"We are dealing with something actually rooted in history," he says— and I must agree.

Something happened after Jesus died.

Of course, Ehrman and I would still disagree when it comes to *what* actually happened and to the meaning of those events.[2] Yet, even in my most skeptical moments, I cannot find it in myself to deny that something *did* happen, and this something did not merely occur in someone's spiritual imagination. It is deeply rooted in the soil of human history.

When I look carefully at the function of crucifixion in the ancient world, I become even more convinced that what happened at the empty tomb was nothing short of miraculous. In the first century A.D., crucifixion represented the darkest possible path to death. The Roman philosopher Seneca described what he witnessed at a crucifixion in this way: "I see the stakes there—not of one kind but of many. Some victims are placed head down; some have spikes driven through their genitals; others have their arms stretched out on the gibbet."[3] Beginning in the third century B.C., the very word *crucify* was a vulgarism that did not pass freely between the lips of cultured people. In one ancient document, a Roman prostitute hurled this insult—perhaps the lewdest sentence in her vocabulary—at an uncouth patron: "Go get yourself crucified!"[4]

No wonder, then, that first-century folk referred to the worship of a crucified God as *mōria, mania* and *amentia*—"foolishness," "insanity" (in Greek) and "idiocy" (in Latin). In fact, one of the earliest graphical depictions of such worship is a bit of second-century graffiti, uncovered near Rome in a palace where slaves trained to serve the imperial family.

In this graffito, a man with the head of an ass dangles naked from a cross. At the foot of the cross, someone kneels, surrounded by these rough-scrawled words: *Alexamenos sebete theon,* "Alexamenos worships God."[5] Evidently, someone—perhaps a servant training to serve

This crude sketch, known as the Alexamenos Graffito, was probably drawn near the end of the second century.

Caesar himself—was ridiculing a young man named Alexamenos because Alexamenos had embraced a new religion, a faith centered on a deity who suffered the punishment for humanity's sin on a cross. From my perspective, in such a world—a world where crucifixion could so easily turn into a vulgar mockery—only an event as amazing as resurrection can explain why the first followers of Jesus so readily gave up their lives in the name of a crucified God.

A couple of years ago, *The Da Vinci Codebreaker*—a book I cowrote with my friend Jim Garlow—hit the bestseller lists about the same time that Sony Pictures released the movie *The Da Vinci Code.* As a result, nearly one hundred television and radio stations interviewed one or both of us in the space of two or three weeks. I don't remember most of the questions I answered during those couple of weeks, but I do recall one query that came up more than once.

The question came from well-intentioned Christians, and it went something like this: "Why do you think Dan Brown, author of *The Da Vinci Code,* is such a threat to the Christian faith?"

"He isn't," was my response, and the subsequent moment of awkward silence informed me that this wasn't quite the answer the host expected. So I continued, "Jesus said that no external threats—not even the 'gates of Hades,' to use his words—could stand against the fellowship of people that claims his name. If the gates of Hades pose no ultimate threat to Christian faith, somehow I suspect that Dan Brown doesn't either."

"So . . . if Dan Brown isn't a threat to Christian faith," the host deliberated, "why did you write this book?"

"Because the real danger *isn't* Dan Brown," I replied. "The real danger is our own ignorance of how Christianity as we know it came into existence. I've spoken to hundreds, probably thousands, of sincere believers in Jesus who assume that Christian faith—and not simply Christian faith, but Christianity as *they* know it, perceive it and practice it—came directly from heaven bound in black leather, with the words of Jesus already lettered in red. They can't handle the idea that the faith they practice was hammered out over centuries of time by hundreds of people—and that at least a few of these people possessed motives that weren't particularly pure.

"When a phenomenon like *The Da Vinci Code* hits the market, Christians who don't know how the faith has been handed down . . . well, they don't know what to do. Some of them see that Dan Brown has raised valid questions, but they can't see the flaws in what he says; so, they believe it and walk away from Christian faith. Others aren't willing even to consider the questions he raises; so, they want to burn his books. I don't believe *The Da Vinci Code,* but I don't want to burn it either. For me, it provides a chance to help people grapple with a real and authentic danger—and that danger isn't Dan Brown or *The Da Vinci Code.* It's faith that refuses to deal with tough questions about the church's history and about Scripture. What *The Da Vinci Code* has provided is an opportunity to help millions of people to begin asking these questions."

I feel the same way about Bart Ehrman and his books. Do I deeply disagree with many of his interpretations of the historical data? Certainly! And yet, Ehrman poses no ultimate threat to Christian faith. What he poses is an opportunity for believers to become more aware of the beautiful struggles by which God brought us to where we are today. Ehrman has created an opportunity for us to ask difficult questions—questions like, What do I really mean when I say that the Bible is God's Word? and What are we actually claiming when we declare that the Scriptures are without error?

◆   ◆   ◆

A recent *Washington Post* article described Ehrman as having "peered so hard into the origins of Christianity that he lost his faith altogether."[6] It is not my place to psychoanalyze Ehrman or to criticize those that trained him. And yet, it appears to me that the problem was *not* that he peered too deeply into the origins of Christian faith; it was that he inherited a theological system from well-meaning evangelical Christians that allowed little—if any—space for questions, variations or rough edges.[7] Scripture was assumed to be divine in such a way that no place remained for the human aspects of the Bible's creation, conservation and canonization.

Faced with the inescapable humanness of Scripture, he found that the theological categories he had inherited from his teachers no longer worked. So, Ehrman abandoned his belief in the inerrancy of Scripture. In a review of Ehrman's *Misquoting Jesus,* New Testament scholar Robert Gundry put it this way:

> [Ehrman] makes quite clear his further and ultimate purpose . . . to proclaim New Testament textual criticism as bad news to all who believe the Bible to be God's Word. Thus Ehrman's leading question to such believers: "What if the book you take as giving you God's words instead contains human words?" There's the rub: Ehrman has so hardened the categories of humanity and divinity that since the Bible is "a very human book," for him it can't also be divinely inspired. The human authors' writing out of their "needs, beliefs, worldviews, opinions, loves, hates, longings, desires, situations, problems" somehow excludes the Holy Spirit's using those needs, beliefs, worldviews, and so on to convey divine revelation. As though God could have communicated in a vacuum, apart from such concomitants! . . . No wonder, then, that Ehrman's "journey" from evangelicalism came to what he calls "a dead end." His evangelical faith died by way of a hardening of the categories; and his self-reported post-mortem stands as a warning to evangelicals, from whom he inherited some of that hardening of categories.[8]

◆   ◆   ◆

Though I mourn the death of Ehrman's faith, I must admit that he has raised many fruitful questions—questions that cannot be blithely ignored. Consequently, the most appropriate response is *not* to iden-

THINK IT OUT

"Bart was, like a lot of people who were converted to fundamental evangelicalism, converted to the certainty of it all, of having all the answers. When he found out they were lying to him, he just didn't want anything to do with it. His wife and I go to Mass sometimes. He never comes with us anymore."[9]

Dr. Dale Martin
Friend of Bart D. Ehrman

tify Ehrman as the enemy. Neither is it to attack his ideas with oversimplified zeal. Nearly thirty years ago, evangelical scholar J. I. Packer commented,

It will be sad if zeal for inerrancy entrenches a wholly backward-looking bibliology. Fruitful questions thrown up in the liberal camp . . . await evangelical exploration, which as yet they have hardly had. The battle for the Bible must continue as long as unbelieving babble about the Bible continues, but as Archbishop Michael Ramsey once said: "the best defense of any doctrine is the creative exposition of it," and the creative exposition of the doctrine of Scripture requires work on these questions which still waits to be taken in hand.[10]

The best defense of any doctrine is the creative exposition of it. I kept those words in front of me throughout the time that I wrote this book. Why? Because I deeply believe that the best response to Ehrman *is* to wrestle creatively with the questions that his books raise.

Whether I have succeeded in crafting a creative exposition in these

---

THINK IT OUT

"I would love for him to be there with me [at church] and sometimes wish it was something we share. But I respect the integrity of decisions he's made, even if I reject the logic by which he reached them."[11]

Dr. Sarah Beckwith
Bart Ehrman's wife

---

pages, I cannot tell. That is yours to decide. But this I do know: The more I wrestle with each historical possibility, the more I become convinced that—though there is much I do not know and there are some truths I cannot reconcile—Christian faith is no dead end.

At some point where the horizons of faith and history ever so gingerly embrace one another, I still find myself unable to escape this conviction: The tomb was empty because what appeared to be the end of the story was actually the birth of a new beginning, because death turned into life, because what was least probable of all became possible and real and true. What's more, I believe the New Testament includes testimony from the women and men who first witnessed the results of this reversal. Nothing less can account for the evidence I find not only in Scripture but also beyond the Scriptures, in the testimony of the church's first four centuries. It simply "fits the lock."[12]

APPENDIX

How Valuable Is the Testimony of Papias?

At several points in *Misquoting Truth,* I have appealed to the frag-
mentary writings of a church leader from the early second century,
Papias of Hierapolis. In *Peter, Paul, and Mary Magdalene,* Ehrman
makes the following claim regarding the writings of Papias:

> There's an even bigger problem with taking Papias at his word
> when he indicates that Mark's Gospel is based on an eyewitness
> report of Peter: virtually everything else that Papias says is
> widely, and rightly, discounted by scholars as pious imagination
> rather than historical fact.[1]

In fairness to Ehrman's position, some early Christian theologians
did engage in pious—as well as, in the descriptions of the heretical
Carpocratians in the writings of Clement of Alexandria and Epipha-
nius of Salamis, quite *impious*[2]—imaginings.

Still, Ehrman's own declaration at this point is, I think, a bit of an
overstatement. The fragments of Papias's writings include stories
about a man named Justus Barsabas who was poisoned but didn't die
and about a dead man who was raised to life.[3] Papias also described
traditions, allegedly from John the author of Revelation, about a future epoch of earthly bliss and material blessings following the return
of Jesus to earth ("the millennium"). Such ideas may strike some persons as odd, but they do not differ significantly from notions that
were already present in the New Testament.

Papias *did* record at least one tradition that could qualify as "pious imagination." Recounting the death of Judas Iscariot, Papias recorded a story in which the betrayer—apparently having survived the suicide attempt described in Matthew 27:5—swelled until his eyes could not be seen and his genitals oozed putrid pus. In the end, Judas died on his own land in such a way that the entire property stank; this account seems to expand on the tradition found in Acts 1:18. Although scholars in previous generations were hesitant to ascribe this story to Papias,[4] it appears—based on the report recorded in the writings of Apollinarius of Laodicea—that Papias *may* actually have preserved this tale about Judas. Responding to the tale of Judas's death, Ehrman comments that "Papias was obviously given to flights of fancy."[5]

So what effect do these stories have on the tradition that Papias preserved regarding the Gospels According to Matthew and Mark?

Very little, really.

The importance of Papias's testimony is that it verifies that the type of authorial traditions cited by Irenaeus of Lyons—traditions that connected the four New Testament Gospels to Matthew, Mark, Luke and John—existed long before the mid to late second century. Through what remains of Papias's writings, it is clear that these traditions were at least as ancient as the late first or early second century.

Papias faithfully recorded stories that he heard, and it is possible that some of these stories were exaggerated. But the fact that Papias *may* have recorded some exaggerated stories does not negate the crucial fact that he recorded oral traditions about the Gospels that were in circulation fewer than twenty years after the last of the four New Testament Gospels was written. This fact is already suggested by the consistency with which the various manuscripts connect the four Gospels to the same authors; the testimony of Papias simply confirms this suggestion.

ACKNOWLEDGMENTS

Misquoting *Truth* is the direct result of approximately 132 mocha lattes. I consumed these potables in front of the fireplace at the finest Starbucks in the world—Jim Misch's store on Yale Avenue in Tulsa, Oklahoma—and at the Nordaggio's coffee shops in Tulsa, Owasso and Jenks. Thanks to the many baristas who allowed me to remain in their stores long after my presence officially qualified as loitering.

The pathway that led to this book began in 2005 when Jim Garlow invited me to write *The Da Vinci Codebreaker* with him. Researching *The Da Vinci Codebreaker* led me to the writings of Bart Ehrman, and what I read in Ehrman's books drove me to write this response. Thank you, Jim, for your partnership and encouragement. Mike Nappa at Nappaland Literary Agency found precisely the right publisher to bring the book to you. I am privileged to have worked with the outstanding people at InterVarsity Press, especially my editor Jim Hoover. In Jim, InterVarsity Press provided not only an excellent editor but also an accomplished fellow scholar. Helena Rivera Navarro assisted me in my research by translating portions of Ivo Tamm's German thesis into English. Darrell L. Bock, Robert H. Gundry, Robert Yarbrough and Peter Jones took the time to correspond about specific questions regarding the titles of the Gospels and the fate of the autographs. First Baptist Church of Rolling Hills graciously granted a thirty-day sabbatical from executive duties so that I could complete this book—special thanks to administrative assistant Lily Lovett and associate ministers Brad Brooks and Jeremy Goggans for taking care of business in my absence.

What compelled me most strongly to complete this book as quickly as possibly was not, however, any deadline or editor or agent. It was the fact that God has gifted me with two beautiful girls who welcome me home each night and who believe in me even when I fail to believe in myself. When I think of the two of you, words can no longer bear the weight of what I feel. There are no sentences to describe this love. There is only the catch in my throat each time I look into your eyes and the fathomless yearning in my heart each moment that we are apart. To my wife, Rayann, and my daughter, Hannah, thank you . . . thank you for loving this cranky, overdriven writer who adores you more than words can say.

Still learning to be God's child,
Timothy Paul Jones

ABOUT THE AUTHOR

In addition to bachelor's and master's degrees in biblical literature and pastoral ministry, Timothy Paul Jones has earned a research doctorate from The Southern Baptist Theological Seminary. His doctoral dissertation challenged the linguistic basis of Wilfred Cantwell Smith's argument for the possibility of a faith that requires no objective content and examined the statistical relationship between Christian faith-development and transreligious spirituality.

Dr. Jones is the recipient of numerous awards for his research and writing, including the Baker Book House Award for excellence in theological studies and—for his doctoral work in the field of faith development—the North American Professors of Christian Education Scholastic Recognition Award. In 2003, *Christianity Today Online* selected *Christian History Made Easy* for its listing of the Top Ten Entry Points to Christian History. In 2005, the readers of LifeWay.com selected *Finding God in a Galaxy Far, Far Away* as a Reader's Choice Best Book of the Year.

Besides *Misquoting Truth*, Dr. Jones has authored *Christian History Made Easy* (Rose Publishing), *Finding God in a Galaxy Far, Far Away* (Waterbrook Multnomah), *Answers to "The Da Vinci Code"* (Rose Publishing), *Prayers Jesus Prayed* (Servant Publications), *Praying Like the Jew, Jesus* (Messianic Jewish Publications) and *Discovering God's Glory in Ordinary Life* (Cook Communications). His articles have appeared in *Discipleship Journal, Leading Adults, Preaching, Biblical Illus-*

trator, *Perspectives in Religious Studies, Religious Education, Christian Education Journal, Bibliotheca Sacra* and *Midwestern Journal of Theology.* Dr. Jones also coauthored the bestselling *The Da Vinci Codebreaker* (Bethany House) and contributed more than two hundred entries to two popular reference works, *Nelson's New Christian Dictionary* and *Nelson's Dictionary of Christianity* (Thomas Nelson). Nearly a half million of his books and pamphlets are in print around the world.

Timothy Paul Jones is currently the Senior Pastor of First Baptist Church of Rolling Hills, a mission-focused congregation on the outskirts of Tulsa, Oklahoma. He has also served Midwestern Baptist Theological Seminary and Oklahoma Baptist University's Seminary Extension program as a visiting professor of biblical languages.

Dr. Jones has been married to his wife, Rayann, since 1994. In 2003, they became the adoptive parents of Hannah, a seven-year-old girl from Romania. Hannah and her daddy spend their evenings playing *Star Wars* Attacktix on the dining room table and chasing each other around the house with lightsabers until Darth Mommy sends them outside. The Jones family resides in Catoosa, Oklahoma, in a house owned by two cats, Martin Luther and Shadowfax, and a Siberian Husky named Remus Lupin.

NOTES

Introduction: A New Breed of Biblical Scholar?

[1]Jeanette Leardi, "Q&A with Bible Historian Bart Ehrman," in *The Dallas Morning News* (July 29, 2006): retrieved February 2, 2007, from <http://www.krue.com/sharedcontent/dws/dn/religion/stories/DN-Q&Aehrman_29rel.APT.State.Edition1.25027f3.html>.

[2]See Daniel B. Wallace, "The Gospel According to Bart," *Journal of the Evangelical Theological Society* 49 (June 2006): 327.

[3]Bart D. Ehrman, *Misquoting Jesus: The Story Behind Who Changed the Bible and Why* (New York: HarperCollins, 2005), pp. 7, 10-11. Hereafter, *Misquoting Jesus* will be cited as *MJ*, followed by the page numbers.

[4]Ibid., pp. 7, 11.

[5]Bart D. Ehrman, *Lost Christianities* (New York: Oxford University Press, 2003), pp. 3, 235. Hereafter, *Lost Christianities* will be cited as *LC*, followed by the page numbers. In fact, the Gospel According to John *does* include several "we" statements that were intended to identify the source of the Gospel as a companion of Jesus (Richard Bauckham, *Jesus and the Eyewitnesses: The Gospels as Eyewitness Testimony* [Grand Rapids, Mich.: Eerdmans, 2006], pp. 369-83).

[6]*MJ*, p. 11.

[7]C. S. Lewis, "Answers to Questions on Christianity" and "Myth Became Fact," in *God in the Dock: Essays on Theology and Ethics,* ed. Walter Hooper (Grand Rapids, Mich.: Eerdmans, 1970), pp. 58, 66.

[8]*MJ*, p. 3.

[9]Ibid., p. 4.

[10]Ibid., pp. 9-10.

[11]Ibid., p. 3.

[12]See R. T. France, *The Gospel of Mark: A Commentary on the Greek Text* (Grand Rapids, Mich.: Eerdmans, 2002), p. 146. It is still commonly accepted practice to refer to a person by the office or status that he or she ultimately attained. For example, a children's biography of George W. Bush asks, "Where did President Bush attend college?" <http://www.whitehouse.gov/kids/president/>. Even though Bush attended college more than thirty years before becoming president, the title *President* is ascribed at this point because this was the office that he ultimately attained.

[13]Neely Tucker, "The Book of Bart," *Washington Post* (March 5, 2006): retrieved August 22, 2006, from <http://www.washingtonpost.com/ >.

Chapter One: Truth About "The Originals That Matter"

[1]Charles Caldwell Ryrie, *What You Should Know About Inerrancy,* rev. ed. (Chicago, Ill.: Moody Press, 1981), p. 16.

[2]*MJ,* pp. 7, 11.

[3]E. J. Young, *Thy Word Is Truth* (Grand Rapids, Mich.: Eerdmans, 1957), p. 119. For other sources, see, e.g., Kurt and Barbara Aland, *The Text of the New Testament: An Introduction to the Critical Editions and to the Theory and Practice of Modern Textual Criticism* (Grand Rapids, Mich.: Eerdmans, 1989), p. 51.

[4]For rhetorical rationale for the accuracy of the Gospels in comparison with other ancient works, see A. R. Millard, *Reading and Writing in the Time of Jesus* (New York: New York University Press, 2000), pp. 227-29.

[5]*MJ,* p. 90.

[6]Ehrman cites two excellent works on the subject of literacy in the ancient world—William V. Harris, *Ancient Literacy* (Cambridge, Mass.: Harvard University Press, 1989), and Catherine Hezser, *Jewish Literacy in Roman Palestine* (Tübingen: Mohr [Siebeck], 2001). See especially pages 326-31 in Harris's book. To this list, I would add Teresa Morgan, *Literate Education in the Hellenistic and Roman Worlds* (Cambridge: Cambridge University Press, 1999). For a more optimistic perspective than one finds in these texts, see Millard, *Reading and Writing,* pp. 154-85.

[7]*Passio Sanctorum Scillitanorum*: retrieved October 28, 2006, from <http://www.let.kun.nl/ V.Hunink/ONDERWIJS/documents/OCHR_actascill.pdf >.

[8]Recognizing that Jesus was actually born *before* A.D. 1, many scholars have replaced the familiar B.C./A.D. designations with B.C.E. ("Before the Christian Era" or "Before the Common Era") and C.E. ("Christian Era" or "Common Era"). In either case, however, Jesus of Nazareth remains the demarcation point of calendars in the Western world; this book retains the traditional designations B.C. ("Before Christ") and A.D. (Latin *Anno Domini,* "Lord's Year"). Because Jesus was born during the reign of Herod the Great (Matthew 2–3) and Herod the Great was thought to have died around 4 B.C., the suggested date for Jesus' birth has traditionally been 5 or 4 B.C. However, recent studies have shown that Herod may have died as late as 1 B.C., expanding the possible range of dates for Jesus' birth. See David W. Beyer, *Josephus Re-Examined: Unraveling the Twenty-Second Year of Tiberius* (Macon, Ga.: Mercer University Press, 1998).

[9]Martin Hengel, *Studies in the Gospel of Mark* (Eugene, Ore.: Wipf and Stock, 2003), pp. 77-84; see also Mary Helene Pages, *Ancient Greek and Roman Libraries,* M.A. thesis, Catholic University of America, 1963.

[10]H. Gregory Snyder, *Teachers and Texts in the Ancient World: Philosophers, Jews and Christians* (London: Routledge, 2000), p. 178.

[11]For analysis of storage systems in ancient private and public libraries, see Lora Lee Johnson, *The Hellenistic and Roman Library: Studies Pertaining to Their Architectural Form,* Ph.D. dissertation, Brown University, 1984, and Elzbieta Makowiecka, *The Origin and Evolution of Architectural Form of Roman Library: Studia Antiqua* (Warsaw: Wydawnictwa Uniwersytetu Warszawskiego, 1978).

[12]"Often a blank sheet was left at the outer end to protect the text and, in Roman times, a tag

of papyrus or parchment sewn to it to bear the title of the work" (Millard, *Reading and Writing*, p. 24). "Labels appeared on all possible surfaces: edges, covers, and spines" (Jocelyn Penny Small, *Wax Tablets of the Mind: Cognitive Studies of Memory and Literacy in Classical Antiquity* [New York: Routledge, 1997], p. 50). "Finding [documents was] facilitated by the *tituli* hanging from the rolls" (Pages, *Ancient Greek and Roman Libraries*, p. 135; cf. H. Y. Gamble, *Books and Readers in the Early Church* [New Haven, Conn.: Yale University Press, 1995], p. 48). Over hundreds of years, such a tag would be easily lost, so it is possible that the New Testament writings bore titles far earlier than the available evidence suggests. Still, however fascinating such a supposition may be, it remains mere conjecture.

[13]Martin Hengel, *The Four Gospels and the One Gospel of Jesus Christ*, trans. John Bowden (Harrisburg, Penn.: Trinity Press, 2000), pp. 116-18. It seems probable that 2 Timothy 4:13 refers to codices (Millard, *Reading and Writing*, p. 63).

[14]The capacity to place all of Paul's letters in a single book, the desire for Christians to have a form for their Scriptures different from those in Jewish synagogues and the difficulty in obtaining writing materials from the synagogues also probably influenced this transition. See Hengel, *Four Gospels*, pp. 118-20, but also compare Peter Katz, "The Early Christians' Use of Codices Instead of Rolls," *Journal of Theological Studies* 44 (1945): 63-65.

[15]Hengel, *Four Gospels*, pp. 122-24; Hengel, *Studies*, 78. For the chronological priority of Paul's letters in the process of collection, see Aland and Aland, *Text of the New Testament*, p. 48.

[16]Justin Martyr, *Apologia Prima*, ed. J.-P. Migne, Patrologiae Cursus Completus, Series Graecae 6 (Paris: Lutetiae Parisiorum, 1857-1866), p. 67.

[17]Robert H. Gundry kindly pointed me to this quotation: "Age iam, qui uoles curiositatem melius exercere in negotio salutis tuae, percurre ecclesias apostolicas apud quas ipsae adhuc cathedrae apostolorum suis locis praesident, apud quas ipsae *authenticae litterae* eorum recitantur sonantes uocem et repraesentantes faciem uniuscuiusque" (Tertullian of Carthage, *De Praescriptione Haereticorum* 36.1: retrieved November 4, 2006, from <http://www.tertullian .org/ >). Although *authenticae* could mean "complete copies," it would not make sense for Tertullian to have told his readers to travel to Rome, Thessalonica, Ephesus or Corinth to see these copies; by A.D. 200, complete copies of Paul's letters could be found throughout the Roman Empire. The most natural reading of the term in this context is as a reference to the autographs of these letters.

[18]Millard, *Reading and Writing*, pp. 20, 33-34.

[19]Most early Christian copyists seem to have been commercial scribes, accustomed to producing fiscal, legal and administrative documents. The less ornate style of handwriting, the placement of larger letters at the beginnings of paragraphs and the use of abbreviations for numbers and common words all support this sort of suggestion (Millard, *Reading and Writing*, pp. 69-74).

[20]See Aland and Aland, *Text of the New Testament*, p. 55; Hengel, *Four Gospels*, pp. 28-29; Bruce Metzger and Bart Ehrman, *The Text of the New Testament: Its Transmission, Corruption, and Restoration* (New York: Oxford University Press, 2005), pp. 14-15. Although Metzger and Ehrman assume a post-Constantinian date for the rise of Christian *scriptoria*, they also seem to recognize that some scribal organization existed before this time. It seems unlikely that congregations in urban areas would not have established organized processes for the duplication

of Christian Scriptures. The rise of consistent forms for *nomina sacra* in second-century New Testament manuscripts would seem to indicate some sort of early Christian *scriptorium*. See T. C. Skeat, "Early Christian Book-Production," in *The History of the Bible*, ed. G. W. H. Lampe (Cambridge: Cambridge University Press, 1969), pp. 5-79; David Trobisch, *The First Edition of the New Testament* (Oxford: Oxford University Press, 2000)

[21]Pliny the Younger, *Letters, II, Books 8-10, Panegyricus*, ed. Betty Radice, Loeb Classical Library (Cambridge, Mass.: Harvard University Press, 1969), 10.96-97; Justin Martyr, *Apologia Prima*, p. 67.

Chapter Two: Truth About the Copyists

[1]*MJ*, pp. 38-39.

[2]Origen of Alexandria, *Contra Celsum*, ed. J.-P. Migne, Patrologiae Cursus Completus, Series Graecae 11 (Paris: Lutetiae Parisiorum, 1857-1866), 2.27.

[3]*MJ*, p. 52.

[4]Ibid.

[5]Compare the words of Irenaeus at the end of one of his treatises, preserved in Eusebius *Ecclesiastical History* 5.20.

[6]*MJ*, p. 89; Daniel B. Wallace, "The Gospel According to Bart," *Journal of the Evangelical Theological Society* 49 (June 2006): 331.

[7]*MJ*, p. 48.

[8]Ehrman himself seems to recognize this tendency; according to a *Washington Post* article, "he's often on CNN, the Discovery Channel, National Geographic, a scholar amused by 'taking something *really* complicated and getting a sound bite out of it'" (Neely Tucker, "The Book of Bart," *Washington Post* [March 5, 2006]: retrieved August 22, 2006, from <http://www .washingtonpost.com/ >).

[9]Wallace, "Gospel According to Bart," p. 330.

[10]*MJ*, p. 69.

[11]Ibid., p. 62.

[12]Ibid., p. 87.

[13]Michael J. Kruger, Review of *Misquoting Jesus: The Story Behind Who Changed the Bible and Why*, by Bart Ehrman, *Journal of the Evangelical Theological Society* 49 (June 2006): 389.

[14]*MJ*, p. 69.

[15]Ibid., pp. 208, 211.

[16]*LC*, p. 221.

[17]*MJ*, p. 177.

[18]Ibid., p. 56.

[19]F. F. Bruce, *The New Testament Documents: Are They Reliable?* (Downers Grove, Ill.: InterVarsity Press, 1972), p. 20.

Chapter Three: Truth About "Significant Changes" in the New Testament

[1]Throughout chapters three and four, I will refer to information found in the textual apparatus of Eberhard Nestle et al., *Novum Testamentum Graece*, 27th ed. (Stuttgart: Deutsche Bibelgesellschaft, 1999), as well as Bruce M. Metzger, *Textual Commentary on the Greek New Testa-*

ment, 2nd ed. (Stuttgart: Deutsche Bibelgesellschaft, 1994). I also refer to Ehrman's more extensive treatment of this topic, *The Orthodox Corruption of Scripture: The Effect of Early Christological Controversies on the Text of the New Testament* (Oxford: Oxford University Press, 1993), hereafter cited as *OC,* followed by page numbers. However, since my response in this book is intended for laypeople, I have referenced this academic text only when it is necessary to understand the full breadth of Ehrman's argument.

[2]Ibid., pp. 69, 208.

[3]Ibid., p. 132.

[4]Ibid., p. 62; *LC,* p. 221.

[5]These clear attributions of deity to Jesus Christ run contrary to Ehrman's claim that the New Testament "rarely, *if ever*" attributes deity to Jesus (*MJ,* p. 113, emphasis added). Although the attributions of deity to Jesus may be (arguably) rare, it is hardly fair to imply that there may be *no* such cases.

[6]This approach is at least as old as the third century A.D. The third-century Christian theologian "Origen notices the two readings in Hebrews 2:9 . . . but is not interested in deciding between them, finding spiritual significance in both" (Bruce Metzger and Bart Ehrman, *The Text of the New Testament: Its Transmission, Corruption, and Restoration* [New York: Oxford University Press, 2005], p. 200).

[7]*MJ,* pp. 159-61; *OC,* pp. 61-73.

[8]See the presentation of the evidences in Philip Comfort, *Encountering the Manuscripts: An Introduction to New Testament Paleography and Textual Criticism* (Nashville: Broadman & Holman, 2005), p. 332.

[9]The "vinegar" would have been *posca*—the watered-down, twice-fermented wine drunk by poorer classes and apparently preferred by the Roman army because it allowed soldiers' senses to remain sharp (see Andrew Dalby, *Food in the Ancient World* [London: Routledge, 2003], pp. 270, 343; cf. Leon Morris, *The Gospel According to John* [Grand Rapids, Mich.: Eerdmans, 1971], p. 814).

[10]Craig S. Keener, *A Commentary on the Gospel of Matthew* (Grand Rapids, Mich.: Eerdmans, 1990), pp. 402, 632.

[11]Origen of Alexandria *Contra Celsum* 6.36.

[12]R. T. France, *The Gospel of Mark: A Commentary on the Greek Text* (Grand Rapids, Mich.: Eerdmans, 2002), p. 63. Ben Witherington III suggests that the combination of texts may come from a pre-Markan conflation of expectations of an Elijah-like figure (*The Gospel of Mark: A Socio-Rhetorical Commentary* [Grand Rapids, Mich.: Eerdmans, 2001], p. 71).

[13]See *OC,* pp. 187-92, where Ehrman argues that these words were added to counter Docetic Christology. What is most significant, though, is that these verses simply highlight a truth that is already present throughout Luke's Gospel—the full humanity of Jesus.

[14]Metzger and Ehrman, *Text of the New Testament,* pp. 319-20; Eusebius *Ecclesiastical History* 3.39.

[15]N. Clayton Croy has provided careful, cogent and compelling arguments indicating that, although the verses of Mark 16:9-20 were *not* part of the original Gospel, a longer ending—as well as a longer beginning—*did* exist in the original manuscript. See *The Mutilation of Mark's Gospel* (Nashville: Abingdon, 2003).

[16]Metzger and Ehrman, *Text of the New Testament,* p. 323.

[17]Ibid., p. 327.

[18]Oddly, in *Misquoting Jesus,* Ehrman repeatedly misspells this term as *periblepsis,* which would mean "looking around" instead of "looking beside" (see *MJ,* p. 91).

Chapter Four: Truth About "Misquoting Jesus"

[1]Bruce Metzger and Bart Ehrman, *The Text of the New Testament: Its Transmission, Corruption, and Restoration* (New York: Oxford University Press, 2005), p. 88.

[2]*MJ,* pp. 80-83.

[3]Ibid., p. 149.

[4]Although I do ultimately agree with Ehrman that Junia was a woman, the case is—in all fairness—not quite as clear-cut as Ehrman presents it. For alternative understandings of the text, see Daniel B. Wallace, "Junia Among the Apostles: The Double Identification Problem in Romans 16:7": retrieved December 1, 2006, from <http://www.bible.org/page.php?page_id= 1163>.

[5]See discussion in Metzger and Ehrman, *Text of the New Testament,* pp. 288-90.

[6]Most likely, the text was simply intended to place the same limitations on women as Paul had already placed on tongues-speakers and prophets (see, e.g., Craig S. Keener, *1-2 Corinthians* [Cambridge: Cambridge University Press, 2005], pp. 117-19).

[7]Ehrman incorrectly transliterates this word as *splangnistheis,* though no such Greek word exists (*MJ,* p. 133).

[8]Ibid., p. 132.

[9]The presentation of evidence for *orgistheis* in *MJ* does not really do justice to Ehrman's argument as it is brilliantly presented in "A Leper in the Hands of an Angry Jesus," in *New Testament Greek and Exegesis,* ed. A. M. Donaldson and T. B. Sailors (Grand Rapids, Mich.: Eerdmans, 2003), pp. 77-98—probably one of Ehrman's best articles.

[10]The two words *do* sound similar in the Syriac language and, to a lesser extent, in Aramaic. However, since there is no evidence that Mark originally circulated in written form in either of these languages, any argument based on these possibilities would be sheer speculation.

[11]Peter Jones pointed out to me two additional examples of Mark's presentation of Jesus as a passionate prophet—the use of the two powerful verbs *epitimaō* (also used to describe rebuking of demons) and *phimoō* (more commonly used to describe the muzzling of a wild beast) to describe Jesus' calming of the storm in Mark 4:39.

[12]*MJ,* p. 136.

[13]For a devotional exposition of Mark's Gospel that does not avoid the rougher side of this Gospel, see Mark Galli, *Jesus Mean and Wild: The Unexpected Love of an Untamable God* (Grand Rapids, Mich.: Baker, 2006).

[14]*MJ,* pp. 166-67.

[15]"Dying-for" is a distinctly Jewish concept, while the noble death of a hero predominates in Greco-Roman traditions (Martin Hengel, *The Atonement: The Origins of the Doctrine in the New Testament* [London: SCM Press, 1981]).

[16]*MJ,* pp. 142-43.

[17]Ibid., dust jacket, hardcover edition.

Part Two: Why the Lost Christianities Were Lost

[1]*MJ*, p. 153.

[2]This is, of course, an adaptation of Walter Bauer's classic hypothesis as modified in light of correctives from Helmut Koester and J. M. Robinson. Although I am familiar with Bauer's approach and its flaws, a critique of Bauer stands beyond the scope of this study. For the basis of Ehrman's views, see Walter Bauer, *Orthodoxy and Heresy in Earliest Christianity,* ed. and trans. R. A. Kraft and G. Krodel (London: SCM Press, 1971); James M. Robinson and Helmut Koester, *Trajectories Through Early Christianity* (Philadelphia: Fortress, 1971). For critiques, see Arland J. Hultgren, *The Rise of Normative Christianity* (Minneapolis: Fortress, 1994); B. A. Pearson, *Gnosticism and Christianity in Roman and Coptic Egypt* (London: T & T Clark, 2004); Thomas A. Robinson, *The Bauer Thesis Examined* (Lewiston, N.Y.: Mellen, 1988). For a readable survey and critique of Bauer's hypothesis, see Darrell L. Bock, *The Missing Gospels: Unearthing the Truth Behind Alternative Christianities* (Nashville: Thomas Nelson, 2006), pp. 32-55.

[3]See, for examples, *MJ*, p. 222; Bart Ehrman, *Lost Scriptures: Books That Did Not Make It into the New Testament* (New York: Oxford University Press, 2003), p. 2. Hereafter, *Lost Scriptures* will be cited as *LS*, followed by the page numbers. Cf. Bart Ehrman, *Jesus, Apocalyptic Prophet of the New Millennium* (New York: Oxford University Press, 1999), pp. 44-45. Hereafter, *Jesus, Apocalyptic Prophet of the New Millennium* will be cited as *JApP*, followed by the page numbers.

[4]*LC*, p. 92.

[5]In *The Orthodox Corruption of Scripture,* Ehrman implies that part of this rewriting of the historical record included altering the New Testament documents to fit proto-orthodox theology. For a thorough critique of this hypothesis, see Ivo Tamm, *Theologisch-christologische Varianten in der frühen Überlieferung des Neuen Testaments?* (Magisterarbeit: Westfälische Wilhelms-Universität Münster, 2005): retrieved September 8, 2006, from <http://www.evangelicaltextualcriticism.com/documents/Theologisch-christologischeVarianten_Tamm.pdf />.

[6]*LC*, p. 4.

[7]*JApP*, p. 87.

Chapter Five: Truth About Oral History

[1]I have followed Jan Vansina's helpful distinction between *oral tradition* and *oral history*. For Vansina, oral history *becomes* oral tradition only after the deaths of the eyewitnesses and other contemporary hearers of the original event (Jan Vansina, *Oral Tradition as History* [Madison: University of Wisconsin Press, 1985], pp. 26-29).

[2]Samuel Byrskog, *Story as History—History as Story: The Gospel Tradition in the Context of Ancient Oral History* (Leiden: Brill, 2002), p. 116. See also Jocelyn Penny Small, *Wax Tablets of the Mind: Cognitive Studies of Memory and Literacy in Classical Antiquity* (New York: Routledge, 1997), pp. 177-85; Martin S. Jaffee, *Torah in the Mouth: Writing and Oral Tradition in Palestinian Judaism 200 BCE-400 CE* (Oxford: Oxford University Press, 2001), pp. 32-38.

[3]Quoted in Eusebius, *Ecclesiastical History* 3.39. Papias was not attempting to replace or to disregard the written Gospels. Rather, recognizing the value of oral tradition, he sought to ascertain the best oral witnesses to receive alongside the Gospels. See H. Y. Gamble, *Books and Readers in the Early Church* (New Haven, Conn.: Yale University Press, 1995), pp. 30-31;

A. F. Walls, "Papias and Oral Tradition," *Vigilae Christianae* 21 (1967): 137-40.

[4]Plato, *Epistles*, as quoted in A. R. Millard, *Reading and Writing in the Time of Jesus* (New York: New York University Press, 2000), p. 193. For similar opinions from ancient Jewish culture, see H. Gregory Snyder, *Teachers and Texts in the Ancient World: Philosophers, Jews and Christians* (London: Routledge, 2000), p. 177.

[5]William V. Harris, *Ancient Literacy* (Cambridge, Mass.: Harvard University Press, 1989), pp. 326-31.

[6]Tony M. Lentz, *Orality and Literacy in Hellenic Greece* (Carbondale, Ill.: Southern Illinois University Press, 1989), p. 77. Cf. Eusebius of Caesarea, *Ecclesiastical History, Books I–V*, ed. Kirsopp Lake, Loeb Classical Library (Cambridge, Mass.: Harvard University Press, 1926), 3.39.

[7]See, e.g., Paul J. Achtemeier, "*Omne Verbum Sonat:* The New Testament and the Oral Environment of Late Western Antiquity," *Journal of Biblical Literature* 109 (1990): 3-27.

[8]Kenneth E. Bailey has separated oral history and oral traditioning into three categories—*informal uncontrolled oral tradition* (what one would commonly call "rumor"), *informal controlled oral tradition* (in which the community serves as a collective guardian of the history) and *formal controlled oral tradition* (in which a specific individual or group of individuals guards the integrity of the story) (see Kenneth E. Bailey, "Informal Controlled Oral Tradition and the Synoptic Gospels," *Asia Journal of Theology* 5 [1991]: 34-51). I disagree with Bailey's assertion that accounts of Jesus' life were transmitted as *informal controlled traditions.* The eyewitnesses of events remained the authoritative guardians of these stories until their deaths, by which time the Gospels were being written; thus, these accounts constituted *formal controlled oral traditions.* Still, Bailey's distinctions remain noteworthy.

[9]Bart Ehrman and William Lane Craig, "Is There Historical Evidence for the Resurrection of Jesus? A Debate Between William Lane Craig and Bart Ehrman" (March 28, 2006): retrieved August 1, 2006, from <http://www.holycross.edu/departments/crec/website/resurrection-debate-transcript.pdf >. See also *LS*, p. 2.

[10]Tucker, "Book of Bart."

[11]*JApP*, pp. 47, 52.

[12]Bart Ehrman, *Peter, Paul, and Mary Magdalene: The Followers of Jesus in History and Legend* (New York: Oxford University Press, 2006), p. 259. Hereafter, *Peter, Paul, and Mary Magdalene: The Followers of Jesus in History and Legend* will be cited as *PPM*, followed by the page numbers.

[13]*JApP*, p. 229.

[14]For survey of orality in rabbinic practice, see Millard, *Reading and Writing*, pp. 188-92. For examples of these rabbinic patterns in the teachings of Jesus, see Robert H. Stein, *The Method and Message of Jesus' Teachings*, rev. ed. (Louisville: Westminster John Knox, 1994), pp. 27-32. For examples of oral patterns in Paul's writings, see John Harvey, *Listening to the Text: Oral Patterning in Paul's Letters* (Grand Rapids, Mich.: Baker, 1998).

[15]Ben Witherington III, *The Jesus Quest* (Downers Grove, Ill.: InterVarsity Press, 1995), p. 80. Cf. Vansina, *Oral Tradition*, pp. 15, 190-95. Some remnants of the capacity to preserve oral traditions remain even in the contemporary United States of America. While doing ethnographic research among the Lakota people of North and South Dakota, I heard multiple versions of my favorite Native American tradition—how White Buffalo Calf Woman brought the

first ceremonial pipe to the Native Americans. This story is more than a century old, and none of the storytellers knew the story in written form. Yet their story lines remained remarkably similar, varying from one storyteller to another only in the most inconsequential details.

[16]Philo of Alexandria, *On the Contemplative Life*, in *Volume IX*, ed. F. H. Colson, Loeb Classical Library (Cambridge, Mass.: Harvard University Press, 1941), §§75-77.

[17]See James D. G. Dunn, *Jesus Remembered* (Grand Rapids, Mich.: Eerdmans, 2003), especially pages 192-254.

[18]Some scholars, for substantive reasons rooted in form-critical scholarship, exclude 1 Corinthians 15:6a, 7 from the oral tradition. What matters most in the tradition, however, is the clear reference to Jesus' death and bodily resurrection—and these assertions are present in the tradition whether or not its original form included verses 6a and 7. For discussion, see Kirk R. MacGregor, "1 Corinthians 15:3b-6a, 7 and the Bodily Resurrection of Jesus," *Journal of the Evangelical Theological Society* 49 (June 2006): 225-34.

[19]N. T. Wright, *The Resurrection of the Son of God* (Philadelphia: Fortress, 2003), pp. 318-19. See also the reference to the Hebrew *qibbel* in Raymond F. Collins, *First Corinthians* (Collegeville, Minn.: Liturgical Press, 1999), p. 522.

[20]Joachim Jeremias, *The Eucharistic Words of Jesus* (New York: Scribner, 1966), pp. 100-102.

[21]The repeated word-pattern which "and that" apparently translates is the distinctly Semitic *vav* consecutive. See Pinchas Lapide, *The Resurrection of Jesus: A Jewish Perspective* (Minneapolis: Augsburg, 1983), pp. 98-99; Gordon Fee, *The First Epistle to the Corinthians* (Grand Rapids, Mich.: Eerdmans, 1987), pp. 719, 722-26; Jeremias, *Eucharistic Words*, 101-3.

[22]I am assuming here that the apostle Paul was *not* being deceptive about his experiences when he wrote his letter to the Galatians; Paul was, at the very least, reporting actual events as he perceived and recalled them. For discussion of the various aspects of this passage—including Paul's pledge of truthfulness ("my conscience bearing witness")—see William M. Ramsay, *Historical Commentary on Galatians,* reprint ed. (Grand Rapids, Mich.: Kregel, 1997), pp. 49-50; S. K. Williams, *Galatians* (Nashville: Abingdon, 1997), pp. 48-50.

[23]Definition summarized from Johannes P. Louw and Eugene A. Nida, eds., *Greek-English Lexicon of the New Testament: Based on Semantic Domains,* 2nd ed. (New York: United Bible Societies, 1988). Liddell and Scott provide "inquire into a thing" and "to learn by inquiry" as primary meanings of *historeō* (H. G. Liddell and Robert Scott, *A Greek-English Lexicon,* 9th ed., ed. H. S. Jones and Roderick McKenzie [New York: Oxford University Press, 1996].) If *historeō* is understood to mean that Paul desired to become acquainted with Cephas for the purpose of receiving the oral tradition, this would account for the possible definition of *historeō* as "to make acquaintance" (cf. F. F. Bruce, *Epistle to the Galatians: New International Greek Testament Commentary* [Grand Rapids, Mich.: Eerdmans, 1982], p. 98).

[24]It is probably at this time that Paul also received the oral history that allowed him to declare to the Corinthians and other early Christians what "the Lord" had said. For discussion, see Richard Bauckham, *Jesus and the Eyewitnesses: The Gospels as Eyewitness Testimony* (Grand Rapids, Mich.: Eerdmans, 2006), pp. 264-79.

[25]For further explication of this tradition, see two articles from Gary Habermas, "Resurrection Research from 1975 to the Present: What Are Critical Scholars Saying?" *Journal for the Study of the Historical Jesus* 3 (2005): 135-53, and "Experiences of the Risen Jesus: The Foundational

Historical Issue in the Early Proclamation of the Resurrection," *Dialog: A Journal of Theology* 45 (Fall 2006): 288-97.

[26]Gerd Lüdemann, *The Resurrection of Jesus* (London: SCM Press, 1994), p. 38; Robert W. Funk et al., *The Acts of Jesus* (San Francisco: Polebridge, 1998), p. 454.

[27]A shift in the focus of a story because of a change in context, historical circumstances or eschatological expectations is very different, however, from altering accounts with "reckless abandon," disregarding the actual historical events. See Ehrman, *JApP,* pp. 128-32, for an example of how the emphasis of different texts may shift in light of differing historical expectations. Though I find Ehrman's interpretation of these shifts to be suspect, he is unarguably correct that traditions were molded and remolded in light of varying cultural and contextual circumstances.

[28]Among Jewish rabbis and disciples, variances could occur within a story as it was passed from one person to another, but the essential facts and intent of the story remained the same. See Michael J. Wilkins and J. P. Moreland, eds., *Jesus Under Fire: Modern Scholarship Reinvents the Historical Jesus* (Grand Rapids, Mich.: Zondervan, 1995), p. 32.

Chapter Six: Truth About the Authors of the Gospels

[1]*JApP,* p. 42.

[2]*LC,* p. 235.

[3]*JApP,* pp. 44, 46.

[4]Ibid., pp. 42-43, 248-49.

[5]Ibid., p. 42.

[6]Martin Hengel, *Studies in the Gospel of Mark* (Eugene, Ore.: Wipf and Stock, 2003), p. 65.

[7]*JApP,* p. 42.

[8]A. R. Millard, *Reading and Writing in the Time of Jesus* (New York: New York University Press, 2000), p. 24; Mary Helene Pages, *Ancient Greek and Roman Libraries,* M.A. thesis, Catholic University of America, 1963, p. 135.

[9]See Hengel, *Studies,* 66, as well as the critical apparatus for the titles of the four Gospels in *Novum Testamentum Graece.*

[10]Hengel, *Studies,* pp. 81-82.

[11]*LC,* p. 235.

[12]Hengel, *Studies,* p. 66.

[13]The Easter controversy makes it clear that no universally recognized authority figure existed in the second century. Two bishops of Rome—Anicetus and Victor—tried at different times in the second century A.D. to standardize the date of Easter celebrations among Christians. Yet churches in the eastern half of the Roman Empire—primarily Asia Minor—persisted in celebrating Easter at a time different from the time that it was celebrated by the churches around Rome. The matter was still not settled in the fourth century A.D., as is clear from the proceedings of the Council of Nicaea. For various accounts of this controversy, see Raniero Cantalamessa et al., *Easter in the Early Church: An Anthology of Jewish and Early Christian Texts* (Collegeville, Minn.: Liturgical Press, 1993), pp. 34-37; Eusebius *Ecclesiastical History* 5.23-28; Francis A. Sullivan, *From Apostles to Bishops: The Development of the Episcopacy in the Early Church* (Mahwah, N.J.: Paulist Press, 2001), pp. 140-53.

[14]Three second-century New Testament papyri—$\mathfrak{P}^{46}$, $\mathfrak{P}^{52}$ and $\mathfrak{P}^{90}$—seem to have originated in at least two, perhaps three, different areas of Egypt (Fayum, Busiris and Oxyrhynchus). For New Testament manuscripts to have achieved this degree of distribution in central Egypt— nearly one thousand miles from Rome and more than five hundred miles from Jerusalem— by the early to mid-second century, the Gospels had probably reached most, if not all, primary population centers of the Roman Empire by this time.

[15]See Acts 21:1-9. It was, according to Eusebius, from these prophetesses that Papias received some stories about the apostles (Eusebius *Ecclesiastical History* 3.39).

[16] Quoted in Eusebius *Ecclesiastical History* 3.39.

[17]As Richard Bauckham points out, though Papias probably *wrote* around A.D. 110, the time period that he described must have been around A.D. 80 (*Jesus and the Eyewitnesses: The Gospels as Eyewitness Testimony* [Grand Rapids, Mich.: Eerdmans, 2006], p. 14).

[18]Eusebius *Ecclesiastical History* 5.8.

[19]Eusebius *Ecclesiastical History* 5.20. For a defense of the authenticity of Irenaeus's claims regarding having sat at the feet of Polycarp, see Bauckham, *Jesus and the Eyewitnesses,* pp. 295-96.

[20]Martin Hengel, *The Four Gospels and the One Gospel of Jesus Christ,* trans. John Bowden (Harrisburg, Penn.: Trinity Press, 2000), p. 36.

[21]Claus-Jürgen Thornton, *Der Zeuge des Zeugen: Lukas als Historiker der Paulusreisen* [The Witness of the Witness: Luke as Historian of Paul's Travels], ed. Martin Hengel, Wissenschaftliche Untersuchungen zum Neuen Testament 56 (Tübingen: Mohr [Siebeck], 1991), pp. 10-82.

[22]This merging of Matthew's recollections with Mark's Gospel while translating Matthew's recollections might not have been viewed as the creation of a new work. It would have been viewed as an expanded translation. For more on ancient authors' understanding of "translation," see George Kennedy, "Classical and Christian Source Criticism," in *The Relationships Among the Gospels,* ed. W. O. Walker (San Antonio: Trinity University Press, 1978), p. 144.

[23]George Howard argues that the earlier, Hebraic form of the Gospel According to Matthew may be found in the writings of a Jewish scholar named Shem Tov Ben Isaac, author of a fourteenth-century refutation of the Christian Gospels. See George Howard, *Hebrew Gospel of Matthew* (Macon, Ga.: Mercer University Press, 1995), as well as R. F. Sheddinger, "The Textual Relationship Between $\mathfrak{P}^{45}$ and Shem Tob's Hebrew Matthew," *New Testament Studies* 43 (1997): 58-71.

[24]It seems, as with the Gospel According to Matthew, that the Greek and Aramaic versions were independent documents while still sharing the same content. See Hengel, *Four Gospels,* p. 74.

[25]J. A. Fitzmyer, "4Qpap Tobit[a] ar," in *Qumran Cave 4: VIII Parabiblical Texts 2* (Oxford: Clarendon Press, 1995), pp. 1-76.

Chapter Seven: Truth About Eyewitness Testimony

[1]This document is commonly known as the Muratorian Fragment. It originally included references to Matthew and Mark, but only a fragment of the last sentence of the description of Mark's Gospel remains. The specific reference in the document to the recent death of Pius, overseer of the Roman church, suggests an Italian—probably Roman—provenance. I take the

Latin phrase *ex opinione* in the Muratorian Fragment as equivalent to the Greek *ex akoēs*—
"from that which is heard," that is, an oral tradition. For the text of the Muratorian Fragment,
see Bruce M. Metzger, *The Canon of the New Testament* (Oxford: Clarendon Press, 1987), pp.
305-7. For analysis of the Muratorian Fragment, see Geoffrey Mark Hahneman, *The Muratorian Fragment and the Development of the Canon* (New York: Oxford University Press, 1992).

[2]The Gospel According to Mark does—as Richard Bauckham has pointed out—claim the eyewitness testimony of Simon Peter as its source, but this claim is not stated clearly. It is implied
with great subtlety and literary finesse (*Jesus and the Eyewitnesses: The Gospels as Eyewitness
Testimony* [Grand Rapids, Mich.: Eerdmans, 2006], pp. 124-27).

[3]Irenaeus of Lyons *Adversus Haereses* 3.11.

[4]Justin Martyr, *Dialogus cum Tryphone*, ed. J.-P. Migne, Patrologiae Cursus Completus, Series
Graecae 6 (Paris: Lutetiae Parisiorum, 1857-1866), 103.8; 106.3.

[5]Tertullian of Carthage *Adversus Marcionem* 4.2: retrieved October 28, 2006, from <http://
www.tertullian.org/ >.

[6]For further exposition of the importance of eyewitness testimony among early Christians, see
Martin Hengel, *The Four Gospels and the One Gospel of Jesus Christ*, trans. John Bowden (Harrisburg, Penn.: Trinity Press, 2000), pp. 141-68.

[7]Bart Ehrman and William Lane Craig, "Is There Historical Evidence for the Resurrection of
Jesus? A Debate Between William Lane Craig and Bart Ehrman" (March 28, 2006): retrieved
August 1, 2006, from <http://www.holycross.edu/departments/crec/website/resurrection-
debate-transcript.pdf >.

[8]*LC*, pp. 19-20. Cf. Craig S. Keener, *1-2 Corinthians* [Cambridge: Cambridge University Press,
2005], pp. 42-43; Martin Hengel, *Studies in the Gospel of Mark* (Eugene, Ore.: Wipf and Stock,
2003), pp. 1-30; I. Howard Marshall, *The Gospel of Luke* (Grand Rapids, Mich.: Eerdmans,
1978), pp. 34-35; Leon Morris, *The Gospel According to John* (Grand Rapids, Mich.: Eerdmans,
1995), pp. 25-30.

[9]Ehrman and Craig, "Is There Historical Evidence for the Resurrection of Jesus?"

[10]For further discussion of this point, see Bauckham, *Jesus and the Eyewitnesses*, pp. 8-9.
These eyewitnesses seem to have remained "authoritative living sources of the traditions
up to their deaths" (p. 20). The accounts of Jesus' life were not, then, *informal controlled
oral traditions*, to use Kenneth E. Bailey's categories; they represented *formal controlled oral
history* (Bauckham, *Jesus and the Eyewitnesses*, pp. 252-89; cf. Kenneth E. Bailey, "Informal
Controlled Oral Tradition and the Synoptic Gospels," *Asia Journal of Theology* 5 [1991]:
34-51).

[11]One other comment from Ehrman might be construed as evidence for the lack of eyewitness
testimony: Ehrman cites a third-century philosopher named Porphyry as having written this
statement: "The evangelists were fiction-writers—not observers or eyewitnesses of the life of
Jesus" (*MJ*, p. 199). In this, Ehrman apparently did not examine the original Greek source of
this quotation, relying instead on a blatantly misleading translation from R. J. Hoffmann. In
the actual fragment of Porphyry's writings in which this statement appeared, the term translated "observers or eyewitnesses" is the Greek word for "historian" (*historas*), and the word
translated "fiction-writers" more commonly means "inventors" or "devisers" (*epheuretas*).
What Porphyry claims is, "The evangelists were devisers, not historians of the life of Jesus"—

still a negative statement but one with no connotations regarding the presence or absence of eyewitness testimony.

[12]*JApP*, p. 45. Interestingly, in a later book, Ehrman admits that some New Testament writings "may well have been produced by the original apostles of Jesus" (*LS*, p. 2). Ehrman does not, however, clarify which writings he believes may have been produced by Jesus' first followers.

[13]See discussion and references in Ben Witherington III, *The Acts of the Apostles: A Socio-Rhetorical Commentary* (Grand Rapids, Mich.: Eerdmans, 1998), pp. 195-97.

[14]Alternatively, *agrammatos* could mean that an individual was literate and conversant in a regional language—in this case, the regional tongue would have been Aramaic—but not in Greek. See H. C. Youtie, "*Agrammateus*: An Aspect of Greek Society in Egypt" and "*Bradeos graphon*: Between Literacy and Illiteracy," in *Scriptiunculae*, series 2 (Amsterdam: Hakkert, 1973), pp. 611-51.

[15]In the Gospels According to Mark and Luke, the tax collector is called Levi. Although many commentators have viewed Levi and Matthew as different names for the same individual, this is highly unlikely (see Bauckham, *Jesus and the Eyewitnesses*, pp. 109-11). Given the open-ended and formulaic nature of this account, it is more likely that the individual who rendered the Greek version of the Gospel According to Matthew—knowing that Matthew, the apostolic eyewitness behind the teachings of Jesus preserved in this Gospel, had once been a tax collector—adapted Mark's description of the calling of Levi the tax collector to describe the apostle Matthew. Levi was, it appears, the brother of the apostle known as "James son of Alphaeus" (cf. Mark 2:14; 3:18). There is no reason why Matthew and Levi, both tax collectors, could not have been called in the same manner; after all, Simon, Andrew, James and John appear to have been called in two different encounters in nearly identical ways (Mark 1:16-20).

[16]See, e.g., Epictetus, *Encheiridion*, in *Discourses, Books 3-4. Encheiridion*, ed. W. A. Oldfather, Loeb Classical Library (Cambridge, Mass.: Harvard University Press, 1928), 29.7; Polybius, *The Histories, Volume IV, Books 9-15*, ed. W. R. Paton, Loeb Classical Library (Cambridge, Mass.: Harvard University Press, 1992), 12.13.9.

[17]Josephus, *The Jewish War, Books 1-2*, ed. H. St.-J. Thackeray, Loeb Classical Library (Cambridge, Mass.: Harvard University Press, 1927), 2.14.287.

[18]A. R. Millard, *Reading and Writing in the Time of Jesus* (New York: New York University Press, 2000), pp. 28-29. Some scholars have argued that the apostles were literate and that they would have carried *pinakes* and noted significant sayings of Jesus. It seems to me, however, that this assumes a higher rate of literacy in Galilee and Judea—especially among persons in trades such as fishing—than the available evidence can sustain. For discussion and references, see B. Gerhardsson, *The Origins of the Gospel Traditions* (London: SCM Press, 1979), pp. 68-161, and S. Lieberman, *Hellenism in Jewish Palestine* (New York: JTS, 1962), p. 203.

[19]The abundance of surviving Roman taxation receipts, written in Greek, clearly demonstrates this fact. The epigraphical evidence includes not only brief receipts that follow simple formulas—for examples, see the numerous pieces of Elephantine and Egyptian ostraca in Ulrich Wilken, *Griechische Ostraka aus Aegypten und Nubien* (Manchester, N.H.: Ayer, 1979), and in Friedrich Preisigke et al., *Sammelbuch griechischer Urkunden aus Aegypten* (Berlin: Walter de Gruyter, 1974)—but also more lengthy and complex receipts on papyrus, such as P.Oxy. 51:3609.

[20]Millard, *Reading and Writing,* pp. 31, 170. See the taxation documentation from the pre-Christian era and from the first and second centuries A.D. found in the Oxyrhynchus papyri P.Oxy. 49:3461, P.Oxy. 62:4334, P.Oxy. 24:2413, P.Oxy. 45:3241 and P.Oxy. 66:4527, as well as more extensive contractual agreements such as the third-century P.Oxy. 43:3092.

[21]*JApP,* p. 45.

[22]Philo of Alexandria, *De Specialibus Legibus,* in *Volume VIII,* ed. F. H. Colson, Loeb Classical Library (Cambridge, Mass.: Harvard University Press, 1939), 2.19.

[23]Vivian Nutton, *Ancient Medicine* (New York: Routledge, 2004), p. 69.

[24]Although neither the tasks nor the training of military medics seems to have *required* literacy, Dioscurides—a military medic—was sufficiently literate to author a book describing how to prepare and administer medicines (Millard, *Reading and Writing,* p. 183).

[25]Janet Huskinson, *Experiencing Rome: Culture, Identity, and Power in the Roman Empire* (London: Routledge, 2000), pp. 179-80; Nutton, *Ancient Medicine,* pp. 263-64. For a few of the many documentary examples of literacy among physicians, see P.Mich. 758, P.Oxy. 44:3195, P.Oxy. 45:3245, P.Oxy. 54:3729, P.Oxy. 63:4366, P.Oxy. 63:4370, P.Oxy. 64:4441 and P.Oxy. 66:4529. Though somewhat later than the New Testament era, these documents represent the sorts of correspondence in which first-century physicians might have engaged.

[26]Millard, *Reading and Writing,* pp. 176-85; cf. R. Cribbiore, *Writing, Teachers, and Students in Graeco-Roman Egypt* (Atlanta: Scholars Press, 1996), pp. 1-5.

[27]Ehrman seems to view the fact that a scribe wrote on Paul's behalf as being problematic for persons who embrace the Bible as a book of divine truth (*MJ,* p. 59). However, Paul's use of a scribe does not preclude Paul's position as the source of the epistle; certainly, he would have approved the letter before it was sent.

[28]It is crucial to note that ancient persons were considered to be the writers of a document even if they used a scribe to write the words. Notice how Paul declared "I have written to you" in Romans 15:15, even though Tertius penned the actual document (see Romans 16:22). In the oral culture of the ancient Roman Empire, what scribes apparently recorded was the speaker-writer's oral performance of the document. This performance was then "re-performed" by the courier of the document. See Jocelyn Penny Small, *Wax Tablets of the Mind: Cognitive Studies of Memory and Literacy in Classical Antiquity* (New York: Routledge, 1997), pp. 160-201; H. Gregory Snyder, *Teachers and Texts in the Ancient World: Philosophers, Jews and Christians* (London: Routledge, 2000), pp. 191, 226-27; Rosalind Thomas, *Literacy and Orality in Ancient Greece* (Cambridge: Cambridge University Press, 1992), pp. 36-40, 124-25.

Chapter Eight: Truth About How the Books Were Chosen

[1]*MJ,* p. 36; cf. *LS,* pp. 1-3.

[2]Ehrman places the emergence of this principle later and summarizes it in this way: Authoritative texts had to be "ancient" (from the time of Jesus) and "apostolic" (from the first followers of Jesus or their associates) (*LC,* pp. 242-43). As Ehrman notes, two other standards came into play later, those of catholicity (widespread usage among Christians) and orthodoxy (agreement with other Scriptures). I would contend, though, that—for the earliest Christians—the categories of *orthodoxy, apostolicity* and *antiquity* were not distinguishable. All three categories were rooted in the assumption that eyewitness testimony was authoritative.

[3]Quoted in Eusebius *Ecclesiastical History* 3.39.

[4]Polycarp of Smyrna, *To the Philippians,* in *The Apostolic Fathers, I, I Clement. II Clement. Ignatius. Polycarp. Didache,* ed. Bart Ehrman, Loeb Classical Library (Cambridge, Mass.: Harvard University Press, 2003), 12.1.

[5]Translated from "Muratorian Canon in Latin": retrieved October 28, 2006, from <http://www.earlychristianwritings.com/text/muratorian-latin.html/ >.

[6]Eusebius *Ecclesiastical History* 6.12; cf. Tertullian of Carthage *De Praescriptione Haereticorum* 3.20-21: retrieved October 28, 2006, from <http://www.tertullian.org/ >.

[7]Eusebius *Ecclesiastical History* 6.12.

[8]For further discussion, see Martin Hengel, *The Four Gospels and the One Gospel of Jesus Christ,* trans. John Bowden (Harrisburg, Penn.: Trinity Press, 2000), pp. 12-15.

[9]Translated from text of P.Cair. 10759. For the text of this fragment as well as a more cautionary approach to its identification as the *Gospel of Peter,* see Paul Foster, "Are There Any Early Fragments of the So-Called *Gospel of Peter?*" *New Testament Studies* 52 (2006):1-28.

[10]*LC,* p. 16.

[11]Eusebius *Ecclesiastical History* 6.12.

[12]See *LC,* p. 16. The beginnings of blaming the crucifixion on the Jewish people can be seen in the trial before Pontius Pilate in *Gospel of Peter,* suggesting a date after the expulsion of Christians from the synagogues in the late first century A.D.

[13]P.Cair. 10759.

[14]*LC,* pp. 22-28.

[15]It is possible that Eusebius's *rejection* of *Gospel of Peter* could be construed to suggest that some churches *accepted* the document—but this is merely conjectural. Within a few years of the incident in Rhossus, the fourfold Gospel of Matthew, Mark, Luke and John seems to have been assumed to constitute the authentic and apostolic recounting of Jesus' life. Irenaeus of Lyons had already made this argument around A.D. 180; by the time of Clement of Alexandria in the early third century, the fourfold Gospel seems to be assumed in Alexandria too (Hengel, *Four Gospels,* pp. 15-19).

[16]For examinations of the authenticity of Tertullian's report, see Jan N. Bremmer, "Magic, Martyrdom, and Women's Liberation," and, A. Hilhorst, "Tertullian on *The Acts of Paul,*" in *The Apocryphal Acts of Paul and Thecla,* ed. Jan N. Bremmer (Kampen: Kok Pharos, 1996), pp. 56-60, 157-61. *Acts of Paul* evidently included three documents that later became known as *Acts of Paul and Thecla, Martyrdom of Paul* and *III Corinthians.*

[17]The approximate date typically assigned to *Acts of Paul* has been A.D. 160, nearly a century after Paul. Hilhorst has adduced evidence from the writings of Jerome to suggest a date closer to A.D. 100—still a generation after Paul's death ("Tertullian," pp. 158-61).

[18]"Sciant in Asia presbyterum, qui eram scripturam construxit quasi titulo Pauli suo cumulans convictum atque confessum id se *amore Pauli* fecisse et loco decessisse" (Tertullian of Carthage *De Baptismo* 17: retrieved October 28, 2006, from <http://www.tertullian.org/ >).

[19]Tertullian *De Baptismo* 17.

[20]For example, in *2 Clement* 5:2-4, the unknown proclaimer of this sermon appears to be working from a common—and most likely reliable—oral tradition that's also preserved in *Gospel of Peter.*

Concluding Reflections: "It Fits the Lock"

[1]*PPM,* p. 226.

[2]Regarding the resurrection of Jesus, Ehrman has stated, "The resurrection claims are claims that not only that Jesus' body came back alive; it came back alive never to die again. That's a violation of what naturally happens, every day, time after time, millions of times a year. What are the chances of that happening? Well, it'd be a miracle. In other words, it'd be so highly improbable that we can't account for it by natural means. . . . So, by the very nature of the canons of historical research, we can't claim historically that a miracle probably happened. By definition, it probably didn't. And history can only establish what probably did" (Bart Ehrman and William Lane Craig, "Is There Historical Evidence for the Resurrection of Jesus? A Debate Between William Lane Craig and Bart Ehrman" [March 28, 2006]: retrieved August 1, 2006, from <http://www.holycross.edu/departments/crec/website/resurrection-debate-transcript.pdf >). Here, Ehrman makes the claim that, since resurrection is so highly improbable that it would qualify as a miracle, the resurrection of Jesus stands outside the realm of historiographic research and evidence. In response, William Lane Craig advances an argument (based on the work of Richard Swinburne) that, in my view, is even more dubious than Ehrman's—that one can ascribe statistical probabilities to historical events. In response, I would contend that, when consistent and independent testimonies exist for any event, an adequate historiography requires the historian to consider the possibility that the event actually occurred, whether the event was miraculous or non-miraculous. In the case of the resurrection of Jesus, there *are* consistent and independent testimonies of an empty tomb. Consequently, a historical resurrection should be considered as *one* of several possibilities. The historical records that are rooted in eyewitness testimony have led me to view the resurrection as the *probable* cause for the empty tomb. My decision to believe in the resurrection with a high degree of certitude is rooted simultaneously in historical evidence and in a personal choice to view this event through eyes of faith.

[3]Seneca, *De consolatione ad Marciam,* in *Volume II: Moral Essays,* ed. John Basore, Loeb Classical Library (Cambridge, Mass.: Harvard University Press, 1932), 20.3.

[4]Examples are drawn from Martin Hengel, *Crucifixion in the Ancient World and the Folly of the Message of the Cross,* rev. ed (Minneapolis: Augsburg Fortress, 1977).

[5]The graffito seems to be grammatically incorrect—either the plural form of "worship" *(sebete)* appears instead of the singular form *(sebeis)* required by the noun *Alexamenos* or it is a phonetic misspelling of *sebetai* (a third person middle voice form). Since *sebomai* is a deponent verb, the latter seems more likely. For more information regarding the Alexamenos Graffito, begin with Everett Ferguson, *Backgrounds of Early Christianity,* 3rd ed. (Grand Rapids, Mich.: Eerdmans, 2003), pp. 596-97.

[6]Neely Tucker, "The Book of Bart," *Washington Post* [March 5, 2006]: retrieved August 22, 2006, from <http://www.washingtonpost.com/>.

[7]See *JApP,* pp. 29-30, where Ehrman contrasts two possible views of Scripture, with no apparent recognition of the many possibilities *between* and *within* the two extremes: "Jesus' walking on the water is not an actual historical event but a myth—a history-like story that is trying to convey a truth. . . . It's not something that *happened.* It's something that *happens.* . . . Just about the only scholars who disagree are those who, for theological reasons, believe that the Bible

contains the literal, inerrant, inspired, no-mistakes-of-any-kind and no-historical-problems-whatsoever, absolute words directly from God. Everyone else pretty much agrees: the Gospels . . . contain stories that didn't happen as told, which are nonetheless meant to teach a lesson."

[8]Robert H. Gundry, "Post-Mortem: Death by Hardening of the Categories": retrieved February 2, 2007, from <www.christianitytoday.com/bc/2006/005/3.8.html>.

[9]Tucker, "Book of Bart."

[10]James I. Packer, "Battling for the Bible," *Regent College Bulletin* 9.4 (Fall 1979). British spellings have been altered to reflect U.S. patterns.

[11]Tucker, "Book of Bart."

[12]This recognition draws from the "minimal facts" approach suggested by Gary Habermas. See, e.g., Gary Habermas with Michael Licona, *The Case for the Resurrection of Jesus* (Grand Rapids, Mich.: Kregel, 2004).

Appendix

[1]*PPM*, p. 9.

[2]See *LC*, pp. 198-200.

[3]Eusebius *Ecclesiastical History* 3.39.

[4]See, e.g., footnote 11 on page 153 in Alexander Roberts et al., eds., *The Ante-Nicene Fathers*, vol. 1: retrieved November 1, 2006, from <http://books.google.com/>.

[5]*PPM*, p. 10.

Subject Index

Acts of Paul (second-century Christian writing), 131-33, 135, 167

agnosticism (the belief that it isn't possible to know whether God is real), 24-25

Alexamenos Graffito (second-century graffito), 140-41, 168

Alexandria (large Egyptian city known for its library and its lighthouse), 40, 49-50, 60, 69, 81, 115, 123, 135, 147

Alexandrian text family (biblical manuscripts from the area around Alexandria, Egypt), 69

Antioch (Syrian city), 126-29

Apocalypse of Peter (second-century Christian writing), 135

apostles (eyewitnesses commissioned by Jesus to testify about his resurrection), 34-36, 38, 71, 79, 90-91, 96, 99, 101, 110-11, 121-22, 124-26, 132-33

Aramaic (ancient language, similar in appearance to Hebrew), 15, 85, 91-92, 105, 113-14, 117, 158, 163, 165

armarion. *See* book-chest

Authorized Version. *See* King James Version

autograph (original manuscript of a document), 17, 18, 37, 155

B (fourth-century manuscript). *See* Codex Vaticanus

Beth-saida (alternate spelling of Bethesda). *See* Beth-zatha

Beth-zatha (pool of Jerusalem, also known as Beth-saida or Bethesda), 61

book-chest (place where early Christians kept scrolls and codices), 35-37, 102-4, 122, 28

Byzantine text family (biblical manuscripts copied in the eastern half of the ancient Roman Empire), 69

canon (authoritative writings or guidelines), 79, 111, 121, 134-37, 144

Carpocratianism (second-century Gnostic movement), 147

Carthage (North African city, modern Tunis), 37, 110, 126, 132

Codex Bezae (fifth- or sixth-century manuscript, also known as Codex Cantabrigiensis), 44-46, 69, 98

Codex Claromontanus (sixth-century manuscript, significant as a representative of the Western text family and because of a third-century listing of authoritative writings found in the manuscript), 135

codex, codices (stacks of vellum or papyrus, folded and bound to form a book), 32, 35-36, 44-46, 50, 69, 98-99, 104, 128, 135

Codex Sinaiticus (fourth-century manuscript), 45-46, 63, 69, 98

Codex Vaticanus (fourth-century manuscript), 45, 50, 63, 69, 98

Codex Washingtonianus (fourth- or fifth-century manuscript), 98

copyists. *See* scribes

crucifixion (ancient method of execution), 59, 76, 90, 92, 128, 140-41

D, 05. *See* Codex Bezae

D, 06. *See* Codex Claromontanus

Damascus (Syrian city), 92-93.

dittography (type of scribal error), 65

Docetism (belief that Jesus only seemed human), 128-30

Ebionism (belief that Jesus was a human Messiah), 79

Egypt (in the first century A.D., Roman province in northeast Africa), 39, 45, 47, 69, 100, 115, 117, 123, 131, 134, 135

Ephesus (city in Asia Minor), 37, 93, 104

Epistle of Barnabas (late first- or early second-century Christian writing), 122, 135

Galilee (Roman province surrounding the Sea of Galilee, north of Samaria and Perea), 92, 117

Gnosticism (belief that the physical world is inherently evil), 79, 133-34

Gospel of Peter (second-century Christian writing), 127-31, 133, 135, 139

Gospel of Thomas (second-century Gnostic writing), 133, 134, 135

Gospel to the Hebrews (also known as *Gospel of the Hebrews*), 64, 135

Greek (language in which New Testament was written), 15, 36, 43-46, 56, 72-73, 91, 92, 105, 113, 117-18, 121

haplography (type of scribal error), 65

Hierapolis (city in Asia Minor), 84, 102, 110, 125, 147

homoioarcton, homoeoarcton (type of scribal error), 65

homoioteleuton, homoeoteleuton (type of scribal error), 65

homonymity (type of scribal error), 65

inerrancy (description of the degree to which Scripture is truthful), 11, 30-31, 33, 145

Italia, Italy (Roman province along the northern edge of the Mediterranean Sea), 69, 93, 121

Jerusalem (primary city of Judea), 92-94

Judea (Roman province located south of Samaria), 92, 101, 113, 114, 117

King James Version (seventeenth-century translation of the Bible), 18, 19, 21, 69

Laodicea (city in Asia Minor), 135, 148

Latin (ancient language), 45

literacy (capacity to read and write), 34, 36, 39, 113-19

Lyons (city in the Roman province of Gaul, the area now known as "France"), 110, 148

Majority Text. *See* Byzantine text family

Marcionism (second-century movement, following the teachings of Marcion of Sinope), 79, 122-23

Moody Bible Institute (conservative-evangelical educational institution), 16, 22

Muratorian Fragment (second-century listing of writings that Christians considered to be authoritative), 111, 135, 163-64

Nag Hammadi (village in Upper Egypt), 134

North Africa (Roman province in north central Africa), 35, 69, 100, 131, 135

Novum instrumentum Omne. See Textus Receptus

oral history (historical information conveyed orally while eyewitnesses are still living), 85-94, 159

oral tradition (historical information conveyed orally at a time when eyewitnesses are no longer available), 90-91, 102, 109, 111, 119, 129, 148, 159

Oxyrhynchus (Egyptian village), 47, 163, 166

𝔓³⁸ (late second-century manuscript), 69

𝔓⁴⁶ (late second- or early third-century portions of Romans), 163

𝔓⁴⁸ (third-century manuscript), 69

𝔓⁵² (late first- or early second-century fragment of John's Gospel, earliest known portion of New Testament), 47, 163

𝔓⁶⁴ (second-century fragment of Matthew's Gospel), 98

𝔓⁶⁶ (second-century copy of John's Gospel), 45-47, 64, 69

𝔓⁷⁵ (third-century portions from Luke's and John's Gospels), 63, 69

𝔓⁹⁰ (second-century fragment of John's Gospel), 163

papyrus (ancient writing material), 28, 32, 34-35, 45, 47, 115, 117, 118

parablepsis (type of scribal error), 65, 67

permutation (type of scribal error), 65

Pompeii (city in the province of Italia, destroyed in A.D. 79 by a volcano), 49

Princeton Theological Seminary (Presbyterian educational institution), 16, 23

proto-orthodox (early Christians whose beliefs were similar to the ones now reflected in the New Testament), 79-80, 96-99, 129

resurrection (divine restoration of life), 64, 81, 86, 88, 90, 92, 94, 109-110, 121, 128, 130, 141, 146

Rhossus (Syrian city), 127-31

Rome (capital city of the Roman Empire), 37, 93, 103, 109, 110, 111, 114, 117, 122, 123, 125, 135, 140

Rutgers University (educational institution), 24

scribes (ancient copyists of texts), 28-33, 37-77, 117-19

scroll (parchment or vellum document rolled around a piece of wood), 35, 37, 49, 103, 105

Septuagint (Greek translation of Hebrew Scriptures), 36

Shepherd of Hermas (second-century Christian writing), 36, 125-26, 135

Sinope (city in northern Asia Minor), 123

Syria (Roman province, north of Galilee and the Decapolis), 59, 127

Teaching of the Twelve Apostles (second-century church manual, also known as Didache), 122, 135

textual criticism (study of manuscripts for the purpose of reconstructing the original text), 17, 18, 43-48, 54, 59, 65, 69

Textus Receptus (sixteenth-century Greek New Testament compiled by Erasmus), 21, 22, 68-70

uncial (ancient writing style), 45

University of North Carolina–Chapel Hill (educational institution), 11, 16

vellum (ancient writing material), 32,
45
W (biblical manuscript). *See* Codex
Washingtonianus
wax tablet (ancient writing surface), 49,
115

Western text family (biblical
manuscripts copied in Western
Europe and North Africa), 69
Wheaton College (evangelical
educational institution), 16, 22

Greek, Latin and Hebrew Terms

agrammatos (Greek, "unschooled"),
113-14
armarion (Greek, "cabinet"), 35
ʾ*aron* (Hebrew, "shrine"), 35
chariti theou (Greek, "by God's grace"),
58
chōris theou (Greek, "apart from God"),
58
dokein (Greek, "to seem"), 128
ekballō (Greek, "I throw out"), 73
hēmeis (Greek, "we"), 43
historeō (Greek, "to investigate"), 92,
161

hymeis (Greek, "you all"), 43
kyriou (Greek, "[from the] Lord"), 46
orgistheis (Greek, "becoming angry"),
72
paradidōmi (Greek, "I hand over"), 91
paralambanō (Greek, "I receive"), 91
pinax, pinakes (Greek, "tablet,"
"tablets"), 49, 115
scriptio continua (Latin, "continuous
writing"), 42
splanchnistheis (Greek, "feeling
compassion"), 72
theou (Greek, "[from] God"), 46

Name Index

Abiathar, 23-24

Adonis, 19

Andrew, apostle, 84, 101, 125, 135

Apollos, 71

Aquila, 71

Athanasius of Alexandria, 123-24, 136

Attis, 19

Augustus [Gaius Julius Caesar
Octavianus], 109

Beza, Theodore, 46

Brown, Dan, 12, 142, 143

Bruce, F. F., 21

Celsus, Aulus Cornelius, 39, 40

Cephas. *See* Peter, Simon

Claudius [Tiberius Claudius Caesar
Augustus Germanicus], 93

Clement of Alexandria, 147

Clement of Rome, 122

Domitian [Titus Flavius Domitianus],
99, 121

Erasmus, Desiderius, of Rotterdam, 21,
22, 68, 69

Eusebius of Caesarea, 64, 135

Josephus, Flavius, 98, 105 114

Herodotus of Halicarnassus, 98

Horus, 19

Irenaeus of Lyons, 103, 104, 105, 110,
148

John, apostle and elder, 12, 14, 15, 36,
37, 40, 44, 46, 47, 56, 58, 63, 64, 68,
70, 84, 85, 95, 96, 99, 100, 101, 103,
104, 109, 110, 111, 112, 113, 114,
117, 118, 119, 120, 122, 125, 130,
134, 135, 136, 137, 139, 147, 148

Joseph, husband of Mary, 56

Judas Iscariot, 84, 148

Junia/Junias, 71

Justin Martyr, 38, 110

Kenyon, Frederic, Sir, 50

Lewis, C. S., 20

Luke, author of Gospel, 12, 14, 15, 36,
40, 59, 62, 64, 66, 74, 75, 76, 85, 95,
96, 100, 101, 103, 104, 109, 110,
111, 112, 116, 117, 119, 122, 123,
130, 139, 148, 157, 163, 164, 165,
167

Marcion of Sinope, 79, 122, 123

Mark, author of Gospel, 12, 14, 23, 24,
36, 40, 61, 63, 64, 72, 73, 75, 76, 82,
85, 95, 96, 99, 100, 101, 102, 103,
104, 105, 106, 110, 112, 113, 117,
118, 119, 127, 129, 130, 139, 147,
148

Mary Magdalene, 16, 48, 85, 133, 139,
147

Mary, mother of Jesus, 56

Matthew, apostle and author of Gospel,
12, 14, 15, 36, 37, 40, 59, 83, 85, 95,
96, 98, 100, 101, 102, 103, 105, 110,
112, 114, 115, 119, 120, 125, 130,
135, 139, 148

Metzger, Bruce, 21, 46, 64

Mill, John Stuart, 47

Mithras, 18

Moses, 48, 74, 81

Muratori, Ludovico, 111, 135

Nero [Nero Claudius Caesar Augustus
Germanicus], 93, 121

Origen of Alexandria, 40, 41, 49, 50,
60, 81

Osiris, 19

Packer, J. I., 145

Papias of Hierapolis, 9, 84, 102, 103, 104, 105, 110, 125, 147, 148

Paquius Proculus, 49

Paul of Tarsus, apostle, 6, 16, 35, 36, 37, 42, 48, 53, 56, 71, 75, 89, 90, 91, 92, 93, 94, 96, 103, 104, 112, 116, 117, 119, 121, 122, 123, 125, 129, 131, 132, 133, 134, 135, 136, 137, 139, 147

Peter, Simon, apostle, 16, 30, 36, 37, 48, 53, 62, 64, 84, 91, 92, 93, 96, 102, 103, 104, 110, 111, 113, 114, 119, 121, 122, 125, 126, 127, 128, 129, 130, 131, 133, 134, 135, 136, 137, 139, 147, 149

Philip, 57, 84, 125, 133, 134

Philo of Alexandria, 89, 115

Pliny the Younger, 38

Plutarch, Mestrius, 98

Polybius, 98

Polycarp of Smyrna, 104, 125

Priscilla, 71

Rehm, Diane, 12

Serapion of Antioch, 126, 127, 128, 129, 130

Simon Peter. *See* Peter, Simon

Speratus of Scillium, 35

Stewart, Jon, 12

Suetonius, Gaius Tranquillus, 93

Tertullian of Carthage, 37, 110, 126, 132

Thornton, Claus-Jürgen, 104

Scripture Index

Exodus
23:20, 61

Leviticus
13, 74

1 Samuel
21, 24
21:1-6, 23, 24
22:20, 24

1 Chronicles
29:11, 59

Isaiah
11:8, 66
40:3, 61
53:7, 128

Malachi
3:1, 61

Matthew
1:16, 56
1:18-25, 56
2–3, 154
3:17, 60
5:1-7, 90
5:21-47, 90
6:13, 59
9:4-6, 30
11:19, 115
13:55, 60
17:12-13, 56
18:17, 115
24:36, 67
26:27-28, 74
26:29, 60
27, 60
27:5, 148
27:34, 60
27:35, 59
27:50, 128

28:19-20, 70

Mark
1:2, 62, 63
1:11, 60
1:12, 73
1:16-20, 165
1:39, 73
1:41, 72
1:41-42, 72
1:41-43, 72
1:43, 73
1:44, 74
2, 23
2:8-11, 30
2:14, 165
2:26, 23, 24
3:5, 73
3:6, 73
3:16-17, 110
3:18, 165
4:39, 158
5:40, 73
6:3, 60
6:34, 73
8:2, 73
9:22-23, 73
9:23, 73
13:32, 68
14:22-25, 74
15:34, 58
16, 64
16:8, 64
16:9-20, 64, 157
16:18, 64

Luke
1:1-3, 75, 116
1:2, 109
1:26-38, 56
2:5, 56
2:33, 56
3:1, 93

3:22, 59
5:22-24, 30
10:19, 66
11, 59
18:11, 115
22, 74
22:19-20, 74, 75
22:43-44, 62, 74, 76
23:34, 62, 70
24:12, 62
24:24-43, 75

John
1:1, 99
1:6, 44, 46
1:18, 57, 58
3:3, 43
3:16, 58
5:3-4, 61
5:7, 61
7:36, 63
7:53–8:11, 63
19, 59
19:24, 59
19:30, 128
19:35, 109
20:28, 58
21:3-10, 62

Acts
1:18, 148
1:21-26, 124
1:22, 109
2:38-41, 57
4:13, 113
8, 57
8:12, 57
8:37, 57
9, 93
9–12, 93
9:17-20, 57
13–15, 93

13:33, 60
15, 81
15:6–16:5, 124
16–18, 93
16:14-15, 57
16:30-33, 57
17:4, 71
18–21, 93
18:8, 57
18:26, 70
21–28, 93
21:1-9, 163

Romans
15:15, 166
16:7, 71, 158
16:22, 117, 166

1 Corinthians
4–5, 124
9:1-12, 124
11:23-25, 74
14:33, 71
14:34-35, 71
14:40, 71
15, 81
15:1, 94
15:3, 161
15:3-7, 91
15:6, 112, 161

Galatians
1:1-12, 125
1:17, 93
1:18, 92
4:28, 43
6:11, 117

Philippians
2:6, 56

Colossians
1:15, 56

4:14, 116

1 Thessalonians
5:26-27, 125

2 Thessalonians
1, 135

1 Timothy
3:16, 56

2 Timothy
4:11, 116
4:13, 155

Philemon
1:19-21, 117
1:24, 116

Hebrews
1:5, 60
2:9, 58, 157
5:5, 60
13:9, 58
13:11-13, 58

1 Peter
5:12, 117

2 Peter
1, 135
1:2, 135

1 John
4:1-3, 81
5:7-8, 68, 70

Revelation
22:18-19, 41